THE HERMITAGE
LENINGRAD

PICTURE
GALLERY

THE HERMITAGE
LENINGRAD

PICTURE GALLERY

A GUIDE

AURORA ART PUBLISHERS · LENINGRAD

This Guide Book will familiarize you with the largest art collection of the Hermitage — that of Western European paintings, which draws to this museum flocks of tourists from many countries.

Considerations of space make it impossible to refer to every picture displayed at the museum, but the most important and characteristic works and the leading schools of Western European painting are represented. The information contained in this Guide will enable you to make a most interesting and informative tour of the Hermitage picture gallery on your own.

Written in a popular form, the Guide is intended to assist a wide spectrum of art lovers.

Text and selection by Yuri Shapiro

Translated from the Russian by Boris Meerovich

Designed by Irina Tuzova and Vladimir Tokarev

© Aurora Art Publishers, Leningrad, 1989

Г $\dfrac{4903020000\text{-}811}{023(01)\text{-}89}$ 61-89

ISBN 5−7300−0081−2

Contents

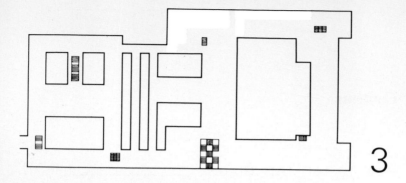

3

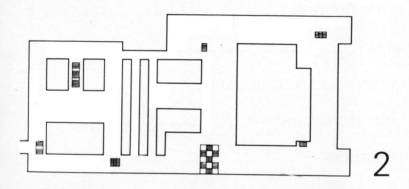

2

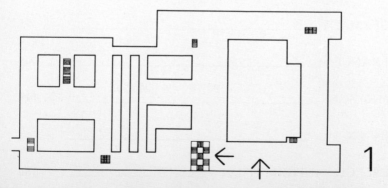

1

How to Use This Guide

This Guide Book consists of eight chapters, each devoted to one of the eight leading Western European schools of painting.

Each chapter is preceded by a plan showing the room numbers in the part of the Museum where the paintings of the given country are displayed.

The name index, to the right of the plan, contains the artists' names preceded by numbers of the rooms in which their paintings are exhibited and followed by illustration numbers.

Illustration numbers (bracketed) in the text are printed in bold type after picture titles.

Room numbers for the pictures (bracketed) are placed under illustrations.

The general name index contains the names of all artists whose works are reproduced in this book.

The history of the Soviet Union's largest treasure-house of cultural and art monuments, the Hermitage, and the way in which its collections took shape, runs parallel, for the most part, with the similar developments in a number of European countries, where world-famous art galleries were created mainly on the basis of exclusive palace collections and Chambers of Curios.

Some of the works of art now kept in the Hermitage were brought to St Petersburg as early as the time of Peter the Great and placed in the first Russian museum — the Chamber of Curios (*Kunstkammer*). But especially many works of art, and particularly paintings, were acquired during the second half of the eighteenth century due to the fact that it became fashionable at the royal courts to collect artistic treasures, an endeavour which, in addition to satisfying aesthetic needs and taste for luxury, helped to increase the prestige of the collector and his or her reputation as an "enlightened ruler".

At the command of Catherine the Great individual works and entire collections were purchased in a number of European countries as soon as they appeared on the market. For this purpose Catherine used as advisers and art experts persons who were genuine connoisseurs of art — the French Encyclo-paedists Denis Diderot and Melchior Grimm, the sculptor Etienne-Maurice Falconet, the noted Russian diplomats Dmitry Golitsyn, Ivan Betskoi, and others. This contributed to the high quality of the collection which included many masterpieces.

The Hermitage is regarded as having been founded in 1764, when the first large and valuable art collection arrived, in Russia, one which was originally put together by the Berlin merchant Gotzkowski for Friedrich II of Prussia. But the Prussian king was unable to acquire it because of financial difficulties, and the collection was handed over to Russia in cancellation of a debt to the Russian treasury. The 225 paintings which it included, mainly by Dutch and Flemish artists, constituted the core of the future museum.

Five years later, in 1769, the collection amassed in Dresden by Count de Brühl, the all-powerful favourite of Augustus III, King of Poland and Elector of Saxony, was acquired. It contained priceless works by Flemish, Dutch and French painters. Three years later, in 1772, nearly 500 canvases were purchased in Paris from the collection of Pierre Crozat, Baron de Thiers, which included works by the greatest Italian, Flemish, Dutch and French masters. An acquisition made in 1779 was a collection which belonged to Sir Robert Walpole, Prime Minister of Great Britain, sold by his heirs, consisting of 198 paintings including those by Rubens, Van Dyck, Snyders and Jordaens, as well as works by well-known Italian, French and English painters.

The last major acquisition made during Catherine's reign was the Paris collection of Count Baudouin which included paintings by Rembrandt, Van Dyck and other great masters (119 canvases in all).

Many works of art initially adorned the interiors of the Winter Palace built between 1754 and 1762 by Bartolommeo Francesco Rastrelli (this is the largest and most important building of the five occupied by the Museum). Erected between 1764 and 1775 was a building later named the Small Hermitage (architects Jean-Baptiste Vallin de la Mothe and

Yuri Velten), which accommodated part of the paintings. Subsequently, when the buildings known as the Old Hermitage (1771—87, architect Yuri Velten) and the New Hermitage (1839—51, architects Leo von Klenze, Vasily Stasov and Nikolai Yefimov) were put up the collection of paintings soon spread to occupy them as well.

Collecting activities continued into the nineteenth and early twentieth centuries. Purchased in 1814 were the Empress Josephine's Malmaison Collection (118 paintings) and the collection of the banker Coesvelt, including works by Velazquez, Zurbarán and other Spanish painters. The museum began to extend also through the acquisition of paintings from Russian collectors. In 1915, the Hermitage obtained the collection of the well-known scholar and traveller Piotr Semionov-Tian-Shansky, which contained paintings of Dutch, Flemish and Netherlandish masters. Though not all the works presented a high level of quality, they enriched the museum stocks with canvases of painters whose names had been missing from the Hermitage's catalogues.

The collections expanded considerably under the years of Soviet power when the museum absorbed paintings from nationalized private collections and from the suburban palaces at Gatchina, Pavlovsk, Peterhof and Pushkin. Many valuable items have been bought from private individuals by a special purchasing commission.

Presently on display and in storage at the Hermitage are more than 7,500 paintings by Western European artists.

The material in this superb collection of paintings is represented, unfortunately, unevenly.

Paintings by artists of the leading Western European schools of the sixteenth to the eighteenth centuries as well as canvases by French masters, beginning with the Impressionists and ending with Matisse and Picasso, are undoubtedly the highest in quality. However the works of Matisse and Picasso can be traced only up to 1914.

Other periods in the history of art are not so well represented in the collection. In fact certain sections have substantial gaps.

The number of Swedish paintings of the eighteenth to twentieth centuries and of Finnish works of the nineteenth and twentieth centuries is quite small, therefore hardly providing an adequate idea about the art in these countries.

Most of the paintings coming from the USA belong to the brush of Rockwell Kent (1882 – 1971), who presented his pictures to the museum (26 canvases). Works by painters of Poland, Czechoslovakia, Hungary and Romania are few and were acquired by chance.

The museum possesses only isolated paintings of Norwegian and Latin American artists.

Expansion of these sections as well as planning and setting up new ones are topical problems facing the Hermitage today and affecting its future collecting activities.

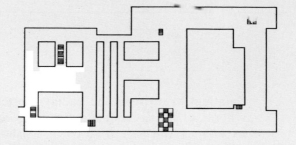

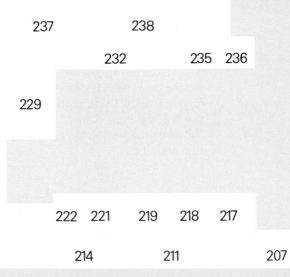

Italy

The Hermitage's collection of Italian painting is one of the largest. The section of High and Late Renaissance art contains works of almost all the great masters. Seventeenth- and eighteenth-century painting is also most completely represented. Other periods, however, have substantial gaps.

An outstanding example of a work by a proto-Renaissance painter is the small panel by Simone Martini (*c.* 1284 – 1344) *The Madonna from the Annunciation* (**1**), executed in tempera. This is the right leaf of a diptych (the left part depicting the Archangel Gabriel is in the National Gallery of Art in Washington). Here the influence of Gothic art can be seen in the lithe elongated figure of the Madonna, in its flatness and S-shaped twist and in the picture's golden background. However Renaissance features are already in evidence as well. The artist emphasizes quite definite human emotions. The Madonna looks startled, her face is thoughtful and grave.

The figure's flowing contours, the festive colour scheme, the amazingly harmonious composition, the meticulous rendering of ornamental motifs done in miniature style, all serve to enhance the grace and elegance of the image created by Martini.

In the rooms of the Hermitage where fifteenth-century painting is displayed two works should be singled out — a fresco by Fra Angelico (1387 – 1455), *The Madonna and Child with Sts Dominic and Thomas Aquinas*, an example of a mural seldom found in museums outside Italy, and a tondo

1 (207)

by Filippino Lippi (*c.* 1457 – 1504) *The Adoration of the Child Christ* (**2**), painted in the mid-1480s in tempera on a panel (later transferred onto a copper plate).

The light figures of the angels in semitransparent robes and that of the Madonna bending adoringly over the infant are full of elegance. The landscape background reveals a knowledge of the laws of aerial perspective. At the same time the artist is in certain ways influenced by the art of the Middle Ages (which is also characteristic of other artists of the Medici circle to which the painter belonged): the figures are elongated, executed on different scales, and depicted at different levels. The painter is concerned not so much with authenticity as with the creation of a definite rhythm and mood.

A decisive role in affirming the new art known to us as the High Renaissance, which lasted from *c*. 1500 to about 1527, was played by such great masters of that epoch as Leonardo da Vinci, Raphael, Michelangelo, Giorgione, and Titian.

The Madonna with a Flower (*The Benois Madonna*) (**3**) by Leonardo da Vinci (1452−1519) was painted in

2 (211)

1478 in Florence where the artist began his creative life. Even in this early work one feels the mature skill and original talent of this great master. Here the child is depicted reaching out for a flower, while the smiling, youthful Madonna looks on, rejoicing at the awakening of his consciousness. The idea of the value of learning about the surrounding

3 (214)

world and the profound meaning of motherhood expressed in this picture contrasts sharply with the ordinary narrative nature of the works of Leonardo's predecessors, masters of the quatrocento.

Having rejected the traditional positioning of the Madonna's figure in the centre of the picture by slightly shifting it to the left (thus achieving greater freedom and a more natural composition), Leonardo places a window at the right of the scene thereby restoring the equilibrium of the masses. In addition to the frontal illumination, coming from the left and slightly from above, traditional for paintings of the time, the light here flows also from the background window, thus rendering depth to the interior.

4 (214)

Not only does the Madonna's appearance — her vestments and a hairdo fashionable in Leonardo's time — but above all, the thought given to anatomy, physiognomics and the proportions of the infant's body endow this traditional scene with a realistic expressiveness never seen before.

The Madonna and Child (*The Litta Madonna*) (**4**) was painted in all probability in Milan to which Leonardo went in 1482. It was through such works that Leonardo asserted for the first time in Italy the style of the High Renaissance. The triangular composition with its symmetrically arranged windows is plain. The figures, illuminated from the front and finely modelled by subtle gradation of light and shade, seem three-dimensional against the dark background of the wall. The Madon-

na's red robe draws attention to the centre of the picture. Though we can hardly see the Madonna's eyes — she is depicted almost in profile, looking down — we sense Mary's tender gaze upon the infant, whose eyes are highly expressive. These very tangible images carry a broad conceptual meaning, reflecting the humanist dreams of the Ideal Man and a Harmonious Life.

The Madonna Conestabile (**5**) executed in *c*. 1504 by Raphael (1483 – 1520) is imbued with an inner harmony and profound lyricism. Peace and contemplation with a touch of sadness on the face of the young Madonna are in tune with the mood engendered by the spring landscape with its distant chain of snow-capped mountains, green meadows and soli-

5 (229)

tary trees along the river banks. The soft lines of the figures so much in conformity with the round shape of the picture; the sombre, subdued colours; the rendering of the airy and transparent distance emphasize still more strongly the kindly solicitude of the mother, the beauty of the world around her.

The other picture by Raphael in the Hermitage, *The Holy Family* (*Madonna with a Beardless Joseph*) (**6**), was painted in 1506. It testifies to the artist's maturity, his penchant for the creation of exalted and idealized images without detracting in any way from naturalness and life-like authenticity.

The first master to have asserted the High Renaissance style in Venice was Giorgione (1478?–1510).

Painted around 1504, Giorgione's *Madonna and Child in a Landscape* (**7**) has many traditional ties with fifteenth-century art: the figures do not blend with the landscape harmoniously enough, the child's movements are constrained, the folds of the garments are unduly complicated, rigid, particularly as they fall across the Madonna's knees. Notwithstanding this, however, the painting clearly displays features characteristic of Giorgione: depiction of Man immersed in thought, an emotive landscape, and rich colouring.

Judith (**8**) is one of the few paintings that can be attributed to Giorgione with absolute confidence. Here the artist addresses the biblical legend

7 (218)

6 (229)

of Judith, who, when the Assyrian army laid siege to her native town of Bethulia, penetrated the camp of Holofernes, the commander of the enemy army, and, left alone with him after a banquet, beheaded the sleepy general with his own sword. Having lost their leader, the enemy retreated. The work's basic idea is a patriotic feat in the name of liberty. Yet Giorgione is a poet with a brush and his image of Judith is, therefore, imbued with poetry. The softly delineated silhouette and, in particular, the harmonious colour scheme with its elegant combination of light blue, wine-rose and pale purple is quite striking. Giorgione manages to convey the finest gradation of colour, so changeable under the effect of light.

The outstanding Venetian artist Lorenzo Lotto (*c.* 1480—1556) is repre-

8 (217)

9 (219)

sented in the Hermitage collection by a family portrait (**9**), which can be interpreted as an allegory for matrimonial faithfulness. This is the reason why instead of painting two separate portraits of the couple, as was usually done by Italian portrait painters, Lotto created just one double portrait. The couple is seen in an interior, sitting on opposite sides of a table covered with a bright Turkish rug. The sitters' faces, turned towards the viewer, lack any spirituality or emotive expressiveness whatsoever. The relations between the personages are revealed by means of the then popular language of allegories and symbols. The man's index finger points at a squirrel (according to a belief current at the time, in a hungry year the male of this animal expels the female from the nest where food is stored). The inscription on the slip of paper in the husband's left hand — *man must never...* — signifies his intention to be faithful. The wife, gently touching her husband's arm, holds a little dog (symbol of loyalty). The two trees beyond the window, swaying in the wind, make the painting's message still clearer.

10 (219)

Of the Hermitage's eight paintings by Titian (1485/90 — 1576) only one is a portrait, though portraiture is a genre in which this painter worked more often than all the other great Renaissance masters. *The Portrait of a Young Woman* (**10**) is typical of his works. One would look in vain for profound characterizations, such as are found in his best male portraits, but the flowery beauty of a sumptuously attired lady is shown to advantage. Her face resembles that of the characters of other works by Titian.

Titian's *Danaë* (**11**) is one of five paintings done by the artist on this subject from Greek mythology. According to the myth, Danaë was the daughter of Acrisius, king of Argos. Taking no chances after it was foretold that he would be killed by his daughter's son, the king shut up Danaë in a bronze tower, dooming her to celibacy. But Zeus, having heard about Danaë's beauty, visited her in the form of golden rain. In the Hermitage version, created between 1546 and 1553, just as in other similar paintings which Titian himself called "poesies", the artist endowed the mythological heroine with features of his contemporaries, Venetian ladies. Beautifully rendered is the nude body: it is at once exalted and imbued with a good deal of eroticism. The theme was popular with Renaissance painters as a vehicle for portraying the female nude.

In his other masterpiece, *The Penitent Mary Magdalene* (**12**), painted in the 1560s, his tribute to feminine beauty and fullness of life is combined with sentiments of anxiety and despair.

11 (221)

12 (221)

just the colour scheme, built on the contrast of dark and purple-yellow tones which intensify the tragic atmosphere of the scene, but even the thick strokes of the paint, applied to the canvas not by a brush but by vigorous finger or palette-knife, all serve to enhance the work's expressiveness.

Among paintings by Titian's younger contemporaries the works of two great masters of the Late Renaissance, Paolo Veronese and Tintoretto, stand out.

13 (221)

The role of the colour scheme in Titian's works is tremendous. As distinct from canvases by Leonardo and Raphael where line and light-and-shade modelling are decisive, here the shape, volume and texture of objects are conveyed by the correlation of colours, whereas the drawing is at times elusive, as, for example, in the rendering of a vessel, even though its materiality seems quite tangible.

In the 1570s, in connection with the general crisis of the ideals of humanism, some tragic notes are sounded in Titian's work. Once one of the most life-asserting artists of the Renaissance, he now creates images filled with drama. In his canvas *St Sebastian* (13) the hero appears as a martyr, spiritually unbroken, yet utterly alone in a sinister and hostile environment. Not

14 (222)

15 (222)

The Lamentation (**14**), dramatic in spirit and expressive in colour, is one of the best paintings by Paolo Veronese (1528 – 1588). Here the artist creates a typically Renaissance balanced composition with large figures. In achieving this he gave up the initially planned image of another angel, as can be seen today with the aid of X-rays.

The painting's colour scheme is elaborated with amazing fineness. The juxtaposition of warm pink and golden tones with greenish-grey ones gives the work a special expressiveness and is in keeping with its theme – the theme of life and death. Despite its small size, the *Adoration of the Magi* (**15**), painted on a copper panel, seems monumental and brings to mind the huge decorative canvases by Veronese, where religious scenes unfold against architectural backgrounds, and the figures are presented dressed in the fine vestments of Venetian nobility.

Veronese was active in the period when the Renaissance was already at its height, and some of his works reflect new principles not at all characteristic of Renaissance art. The subject of *Saul's Conversion* (**16**) is borrowed from the Acts of the Apostles, wherein it is told how the general Saul on his way to arrest some Christians was struck to the ground, blinded by a sudden light from heaven, and he heard the voice of God: "Saul, Saul, why persecutest thou me?", after which he turned into the zealous champion and preacher of Christianity, the Apostle Paul.

The theme of spiritual transfiguration is unusual for the Renaissance, just as are the artistic devices of representing it in the painting. In place of immobility, harmony and clarity we see here chaotic movement, confusion and alarm. Man is no longer the central hero of a work of art, but merely an object in the power of mystical forces. In this picture amidst the mass of figures we notice Saul, who lies prostrate on the ground, only because of a single cool spot — his blue cloak, standing out against the dark warm tones. It is likewise interesting to note that to Saul's face the painter gave his own features.

The Birth of John the Baptist (**17**), a large and important painting by Tintoretto (1518 − 1594), comes from this artist's early period. Yet it already displays those restless rhythms

16 (237)

and dissonances, deliberately distorted proportions of some of the figures, and other features characteristic of the master's later style. On the whole this is a vivid, festively coloured work, permeated with a typically Renaissance zest for the splendour of life and the greatness of man.

This scriptural event is treated as a genre scene. The action unfolds within a wealthy patrician household. Nothing but the glowing nimbus around Mary's head distinguishes her from the other prettily dressed women fussing around the newborn. A wet-nurse is bending over the baby lying on Mary's lap. In the back-

ground of the bedchamber one can see John's mother, Elizabeth. To the right stands his father, Zacharias, addressing a prayer to God. The foreground is cluttered by such prosaic objects as a water basin and a brazier, frequently occurring in Venetian paintings, and there is a cat stealing its way up to a chicken. An earlier variant of the same composition by Tintoretto can be seen in the Church of St Zacharias in Venice.

Hanging on the same wall is a large picture *Jupiter and Io* (**18**) painted by Titian's pupil, the well-known master Lambert Sustris (*c.* 1520 – after 1591), who comes from the

17 (237)

18 (237)

Netherlands. It is based on a mythological subject from Ovid's *Metamorphoses*. The jealous wife of Jupiter,
Juno, having spied from the skies
the daughter of the Argos king
Inachus, Io, in the arms of her
husband, changes the princess into
a white heifer and puts the hun-
dred-eyed giant Argus in charge of
watching her. In this picture, in the
foreground and in the background,
the painter depicted two episodes
separated in time.

The magnificently painted landscape
(which in Venetian painting frequently assumes an importance all its own),
the human figures presented in communion with nature, the rich and

intensive colour scheme — all convey
a feeling of the fullness of life, so
characteristic of Renaissance art. At
the same time, this work bears traits
of Mannerism, subsequently developed in the art of Baroque (the
spiral-like twist of the figures, the
contrasting juxtaposition of the light-
coloured female and swarthy male
figures, and so on).

Caravaggio (1571—1610), a painter
of the Roman school, is represented in the Hermitage by just one
early work *The Lute Player* (**19**),
but it is a picture that belongs
among the greatest masterpieces of
world painting. Though executed
around 1595 by the as yet very

19 (237)

young painter, it already reflects
many features of Caravaggio's tremendous talent.

Wishing to convey a sense of the
substantiality of the surrounding
world, the painter makes use of a
number of innovative devices, depicting his personage and the objects
around him in close-up, utilizing
lateral illumination from an invisible
light source. The dark background
imparts tangible three-dimensionality
to the forms, the finger-board of
the lute is thrust towards the spectator, thus emphasizing its extension
into the space in front of the youth.
The violin is placed on the table at
a tangent with the bow which leans
on it at such an angle as to make
its shadow cast on the table enhance
the illusion of airiness around it.
Despite its genre subject and com-
monplace character, Caravaggio
achieved in this painting true monumentality.

Caravaggio's followers in different
countries borrowed (at times for-
mally) many devices from him. Their
art is quite well represented in the
Hermitage (see, for instance, canvases
by the Genoese painter Bernardo
Strozzi, 1581 – 1644).

The work of the brothers Carracci
(Annibale, Agostino and Ludovico),

founders of Europe's first academy for the training of painters at Bologna, shows their desire to canonize the achievements of Renaissance artists and elaborate on the eternal norms of beauty. As a result truth was frequently sacrificed to falsely conceived ideas of beauty and greatness.

The painting *Holy Women at the Sepulchre* (**20**) by Annibale Carracci (1560 – 1609), executed in the 1590s, is outstanding for its clear-cut composition. Apart from that we see a complete lack of movement; its personages are deprived of any individual features, and their gestures are even theatrical.

Quite in contrast to such paintings is the artist's *Self-portrait* (**21**) done in the same period in a free, unrestrained manner. It shows Carracci's power of observation and great realistic talent, revealed in cases when the painter was able to liberate

21 (232)

20 (237)

his work from the traits of Academism.

Among the well-known Baroque masters represented in the Hermitage collection is Luca Giordano (1632 – 1705), a painter greatly admired by Goethe. The author of about 1,500 pictures (fourteen of them in the Hermitage), he was nicknamed "Luca Fa Presto" (Luke, paint quickly).

The subject of the painting *The Battle of Lapiths and the Centaurs* (**22**) is derived from Ovid's *Metamorphoses*. It depicts the culmination of a battle between Lapiths and the Centaurs who tried to abduct women from a banquet celebrating the wedding of Pirithous to Hippodamia. The spectator's attention

22 (238)

rather than being focused on the central episode of the battle – a fight between Theseus and Eurytus – is attracted by the dynamic composition based on the whirlwind movements of the people depicted. Venus, the goddess of Love, and Mars, the god of war, watch the proceedings from the heavens. The large-scale canvas, bright colours, dynamic movement and engaging content impart to this typically Baroque picture a festive and decorative character. The last great master of the Bolognese school was Giuseppe Maria Crespi (1665 – 1747). He is represented in the museum by a remarkable self-portrait as well as by a number of paintings on genre subjects (*The Death of Joseph, The Washerwoman, Woman Looking for Fleas*). The Venetian school played a leading role in eighteenth-century Italian art. Among its exponents were the outstanding master of decorative painting, Giovanni Battista Tiepolo (1696 – 1770), as well as such eminent artists of the topographically accurate cityscape (*veduta*) as Canaletto, Francesco Guardi and Bernardo Bellotto. *The Triumph of the Emperor* (**24**) by Tiepolo belongs among the works intended for decorating the Palazzo Dolfino in Venice.

The return of the emperor at the head of his army after a victorious campaign is represented in Tiepolo's canvas as an all important event with the column moving right towards the spectator. The painter took into account the specific features of decorative paintings (their function of adorning large wall spaces, their consonance to the richly decorated palace rooms, and the impression they make at a distance). The elongation of the figures placed at the top becomes convincing when viewed from below revealing the artist's intention that the picture be looked at from a definite point. This explains also the absence of small details. The broad painterly manner and a sonorous palette enhance the impression of pompous celebra tion.

Among Tiepolo's best works in the Hermitage is the comparatively small picture of *Maecenas Presenting the Liberal Arts to Emperor Augustus*

24 (238)

23 (236)

(**23**). The majestic personages in festive attire, the architectural background, the bright colours harmonizing with the overall silvery tone, the light shadows, the sensation of airiness — all this resembles the painterly manner of Veronese, who had a great influence on Tiepolo. As Maecenas points out to the emperor the allegorical figures personifying painting, sculpture, architecture and poetry, he directs also the viewer's gaze towards the central group, helping to grasp the meaning of their attributes (a palette, a marble bust, a compass and a trumpet), and

26 (238)

realize that the old man leaning on his guide is no one else but Homer. This work which indirectly lauds the patronage of the arts by Augustus III, King of Poland and Elector of Saxony, at the same time underlines the idea of the freedom and greatness of art, so close to the painter's heart. This painting's idea is so profound that it can easily be imagined on a much greater scale. The interest in cityscapes, that was aroused already during the Renaissance, led by the eighteenth century to the appearance and flowering of an independent genre of topographically accurate townscapes (*veduta*). The best of such pictures in the Hermitage is *The Reception of the French Ambassador in Venice* (**25**) by Canaletto (1697–1768). In addition to a documental recording of the city's architecture with the embankment of the Grand Canal, the Palace of the Doges, the Library of St Mark and the Church of Sta Maria della Salute, it magnificently conveys the rhythm of city life, the festive atmosphere of an official ceremony and the abundance of light, airiness and even the humidity characteristic of a seaside town.

Canaletto's nephew and pupil Bernardo Bellotto (1720–1780), another outstanding *vedutista*, created a whole series of pictures which have recorded for us the beauty of the architectural ensembles of many Italian cities, and also of Dresden, Warsaw, Vienna and Munich.

Bellotto executed the so-called *Royal Series* (views of Dresden and nearly Pirna) for Augustus III, to whom he was court painter for a number of years. Later he repeated the series for his patron Count Brühl, a Minister of Augustus. In 1769, these pictures, as part of Count Brühl's collection, were purchased and brought to Russia.

Of the ten views belonging to the Hermitage (another four are at the Pushkin Museum of Fine Arts in Moscow), on display are *Pirna from the Right Bank of the Elbe* and *The New Market-place in Dresden* (**26**).

The picture *The New Market-place in Dresden* depicts the well-known but no longer surviving Frauenkir-che, Gewandhaus, the guardhouse, and on the left, the still extant building which formerly housed the Dresden Picture Gallery. Riding towards it in a carriage drawn by six horses is the Elector Augustus III. Architectural details are recorded with documental accuracy while people, animals, carriages – all that could be seen in the city streets – are depicted by Bellotto in a free painterly manner. The sense of movement is enhanced by the large contrasting shadows incorporated by the artist.

Though the sky in the painting *View of a Palace Square* (**27**) by Francesco Guardi (1712 – 1793) occupies a tiny portion of the canvas, everything here seems filled with air and light. The spectator's eyes, by-passing the dark arch in the foreground, are directed to the brightly lit palace. The sketchily painted figures, with contours demarcated by light brushstrokes, give the impression of being wrapped in air.

Among the works by twentieth-century Italian artists a prominent place goes to the works of Giorgio Morandi (1890 – 1964) and Renato Guttuso (1912 – 1987).

In his *Still Life* (**29**) Giorgio Morandi, creating a composition filled with harmony and based on a steady rhythm, imparts amazing clarity and lightness to his air-bathed objects painted in light tones.

Rocco and His Son (**28**) by Guttuso is one of the painter's best works in the Hermitage. It is painted in his characteristically expressive manner with turbulent brushstrokes,

27 (235)

28 (337)

29 (337)

generalized modelling of forms and sharp colour contrasts. The work is permeated with a feeling of tragedy and shows the contradictions of the contemporary world. It gives expression to great anxiety, yet at the same time to hope and warm human sentiments as well.

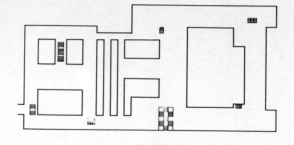

239

240

Spain

The Hermitage possesses one of the world's finest collections of Spanish painting outside Spain. On display here are canvases of all the great masters: El Greco, Ribera, Zurbarán, Velazquez, Murillo, and Goya.

In addition to devotional painting, the late sixteenth and early seventeenth centuries gave recognition to the formal portrait. Juan Pantoja de la Cruz (1553 – 1608) is represented in the Hermitage collection by a characteristic canvas, namely *Portrait of Diego de Villamayor* (**30**), executed in 1605. The seventeen-year-old youth depicted in the portrait, the scion of an ancient noble family, was a member of the Council of State and a knight of the Orden de Alcántara. Its order hangs from a chain on his chest over a costly coat of mail, its ornamentation being rendered in minute detail in the best traditions of Netherlandish art. The knight's armour not only points to the high social standing of the sitter, but conceals also his meagre physique. Despite the desire to elevate the model, Pantoja de la Cruz very accurately, and without ⁓any idealization, conveys the youth's peculiar face – his large aquiline nose, pallid skin and chilling gaze. This profound interest in an authentic presentation of the outward appearance will be further developed in the formal portraits by Velazquez. El Greco (1541 – 1614), the author of the *Apostles Peter and Paul* (**31**), was one of the first in Spain to depict the two apostles together. Despite the disparity of the images as seen in their psychological make-

30 (240)

up, composition and colouring, there is no direct contraposing. Paul, a man of character and spirit, is, nonetheless, no fanatic, his face suggests deep contemplation. A very fine psychological characterization distinguishes the image of Peter as well with his gentle gaze and imploring gesture. El Greco's sympathies, however, are obviously with Paul who, according to tradition, was the one who spread Christianity in the painter's homeland – the Greek island of Crete. Mundane conflicts and spiritual values are reflected in El Greco's picture in different ways in different human characters.

For many years Jusepe de Ribera (1591 – 1652) worked at the court of the Spanish Governors in Naples, and a number of his paintings including those in the Hermitage, *St Sebastian and St Irene* and *St Jerome Listening*

31 (240)

32 (239)

to Trumpets (**32**), show the influence of the painterly techniques of Caravaggio.

According to tradition, St Jerome was depicted either as a man of learning in a cell (working on the translation of the Bible into Latin), or as a hermit. It is the second version that was chosen for the picture in the possession of the Hermitage, one of Ribera's early works painted in 1626. The saint is depicted at the moment when he hears trumpets sounding the Last Judgement. The drama and importance of the events pictured are emphasized by the steep turn of the figure, the sharp contrast of light and shade (the *tenebrismo* manner), and the Spanish painters' general striving towards monumentalism when depicting saints (the low

horizon produces the illusion of raising the figures upwards). The painter pays careful attention to features of nature, faithfully rendering the old man's physique so that there is no mistaking the saint's advanced age.

Originally painted for the Joseph Monastery in Seville, *St Lawrence* (**33**) is one of the best pictures by Francisco de Zurbarán (1598 – 1664) in the possession of the Hermitage. Compositions with the single figure of a saint are characteristic of Spanish art of the time. Martyrs were then usually depicted with the instruments of their martyrdom. For example, St Lawrence, the first deacon of Rome, is depicted with a gridiron on which he was roasted alive. The saint's face is the portrait of a concrete monk; every detail of

33 (239)

34 (239)

his clothing is meticulously rendered, the figure is monumental and sculptural (perhaps the influence of Zurbarán's teacher, a master of sculpture painting). Here is a sturdy and courageous man of the people, confidently standing on earth, and firmly holding the heavy gridiron.

An outstanding Spanish painter of the seventeenth century was Diego Velazquez (1599–1660). Excepting members of the royal family, the Count-Duke Olivares was one of the few whom the artist portrayed many times. Despite the fact that Velazquez was connected with this all-powerful favourite by bonds of friendship, and under the weak monarch the Count-Duke became the country's ruler, in the Hermitage portrait (**34**) painted around 1640, Velazquez shows him without flattery. Behind the smile, outward tranquility and seeming benevolence, one feels Olivares' piercing intelligence and the iron will of an adventurist.

35 (239)

By skillfully changing the direction and character of his brushstrokes, the artist models the face, renders the smooth hair, the bushy moustache, the bluish sheen of the clean-shaven, jutting chin, and the sparkling eyes which seem to be carefully contemplating the viewer. The plain colour scheme with its intense blacks testifies to Velazquez's brilliant gift as a colourist.

At a time when many in Spain preferred paintings on religious subjects to genre scenes, Velazquez turned to the type of painting which was called *bodegones* — paintings of everyday subjects (from *bodega* 'tavern').

In *The Luncheon* (**35**) he depicts three hidalgos at a meal. All three are painted from life (these same models appear in other works by this painter as well). The young man on the right is obviously none other than Velazquez himself. The painter (who was only eighteen at the time) builds up the picture expertly and lucidly. The brightly illuminated white cloth of the table, around which the three men are sitting, helps to arrange and to unite the figures in space. Meanwhile, the sharp contrasts of light and shade enhance the volumes and tangible density of the objects. Arranging every object on the table separately (so that each of them attracts the eye and is well perceived) is a characteristic feature of Spanish still life during the period when this genre flourished.

Bartolomé Esteban Murillo (1617–1682) frequently painted children and did it with great affection. In his

36 (239)

later period, however, he at times idealized these images, giving them a touch of sentimentality. The Hermitage *Boy with a Dog* (**36**) was painted in the 1650s. The chief merit of this kind of pictures is the freshness and cogency of the motif. The seemingly casual pose and the ability to convey light-and-air atmosphere in a landscape attracted to Murillo the attention of the Impressionists.

The Immaculate Conception was one of several popular subjects in seventeenth-century Spanish painting. Murillo, too, treated it repeatedly. Mary was supposed to be depicted in the rays of the sun, standing in a white robe and blue cloak on a moon and crowned with twelve stars. And this is how she appears on a painting by Murillo, now in Budapest. However, in the Hermitage

38 (239)

stage. It was not the actress's performance that attracted him, but her refined elegance and deeply human nature, as well as her tragic fate — she became separated from her husband and later contracted tuberculosis and died at the age of thirty-six, soon after the portrait was completed in 1811. It is the eyes that arrest the viewer's attention in this small, intimate canvas: behind the model's outward calmness, one senses a hidden anxiety. With virtuoso freedom and lightness, characteristic of the painter, he depicted his sitter's headdress and transparent scarf, with its ends hanging in beautiful folds upon her breast.

later version (37) the theme of ascension is central. The gaze and gesture of the young Mary are lifted upwards, her fluttering cloak, the angels streaming in the direction of her movement, the darkened lower part of the picture turning to light as the heavens approach, create an illusion of soaring. Hence the other name of the same painting, *The Ascension*.

The Hermitage has only one picture by the great master of the Spanish school of painting Francisco Goya (1746 – 1828), — the *Portrait of Antonia Zárate* (38). Goya was close to the world of the theatre and frequently portrayed actors and actresses. He painted Antonia Zárate twice (apart from the Hermitage portrait, there is another one in Ireland), and both times not on the

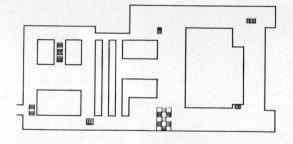

248

262

261

The Netherlands

The Hermitage's collection of Netherlandish art is of considerable interest, even though it lacks works by such great painters as Jan van Eyck, Hans Memling, Hieronymus Bosch, Pieter Brueghel the Elder, and others, and the art of the fifteenth century is represented by a few paintings only.

As early as the thirteenth and fourteenth centuries the rise of industry and commerce placed the Netherlands among the economically developed countries. In the fifteenth century, coinciding with the Renaissance period and the ongoing process of political unification, the country's art strove to reflect life more accurately.

Netherlandish art of the 1420s – '30s is represented by a remarkable work – the diptych consisting of *The Trinity* (**39**) and *The Virgin and Child at the Fireside* (**40**) by the outstanding artist of that time Robert Campin (*c.* 1380 – 1444).

In *The Trinity* one sees a composition which is largely traditional: the modelling of the figures and the representation of the pedestal reveal the influence of Gothic sculpture. The Father, Son and Holy Ghost (the trinity) appear on a neutral background devoid of any depth, in static poses. The sculpted figurines on the throne are symbols characteristic of the religious thinking of the fifteenth century. The pelican, piercing its breast to feed its young, is an allusion to the sacrament of Communion. The statuette of the lioness alludes to the legend where her stillborn cubs would

39 (261)

be awakened to life three days later by the lion's roar (an association with God the Father, who resurrected Christ the Son).

However, on the diptych's other leaf, representing the Virgin and the Child, the master virtually abandons the Gothic tradition. Mary, whose hand shields the infant from the heat of the flames, is placed in the room of an ordinary Netherlandish home in which all the details of the setting are carefully reproduced. Even the nail heads driven into the wooden shutters have not escaped the painter's attention. The basin and pitcher standing on a side-table and the towel hanging beside them –

41 (262)

symbols of the Virgin's purity and innocence – are painted in a realistic manner and are seen, therefore, as nothing more than objects of everyday life.

Interest in the real world, characteristic of the Renaissance, reveals itself differently in Netherlandish art as compared with Italian art: here there is no scientific approach, no theoretical substantiation of method. Painters grope their way empirically, not having mastered, for example, the laws of perspective (the floor is so steeply inclined that the figures seem to be sliding towards the lower edge of the picture), the pitcher, the basin and the side-table are depicted from different points of view. However the Netherlandish masters are ahead of their Italian colleagues in painterly technique. The use of oil paints over a white ground lent to their pigments an exceptional vibrancy and luminosity.

Rogier van der Weyden (*c.* 1399–1464), the author of the Hermitage canvas *St Luke Painting the Virgin* (**41**), was a pupil of Campin. A me-diaeval legend tells us about the Evangelist Luke as the creator of the first image of the Virgin. Shown in the picture is the moment when Mary and the Child are sitting for Luke. However it is not the religious content that determines the painting's imagery. This is a typical work by a master of the Renaissance, a period wherein an interest in Man and a striving to reflect the sur-rounding life become manifest.

Here the painter disposes the figures not in some enclosed space, but

42 (262)

against a broad cityscape background creating a feeling of depth, with virtually documental representation of old Brussels buildings. Another innovation was the depiction of the emotional state of the personages. The painter was able to show Luke's pensive concentration and veneration of his model. Quite possibly, this is the artist's self-portrait.

However, as distinct from the Italians, the Netherlandish master concentrates attention not only on the images of people, but in equal measure on their surroundings. Though all the details of clothing and ornaments are painted with exceptional skill, the folds of the garments are so complicated and broken that it is difficult at times to sense the movement of the body beneath them; the infant's figure is tense and rather elongated; utterly separated are the foreground and background.

Of certain interest is the history of the picture's acquisition by the museum. In 1850, a painting depicting St Luke was purchased for the Hermitage in The Hague, and thirty-four years later another was acquired, depicting Mary and the Child. They were attributed to different artists and only in the Hermitage was it established that they were two parts of a well-known work by Rogier van der Weyden, having been transferred from panels to canvas. By careful

43 (262)

44 (262)

examination one may notice the joining line — the right-hand part is slightly darker than the left.

The sixteenth century was a period of flowering for the Netherlands. It was a time when genre paintings, landscapes and still lifes came into their own.

The well-known painter Jan Gossaert (c. 1478 — c. 1532), following a sojourn in Italy, came out as the founder of Romanism — an Italianate trend in Netherlandish art. In the *Descent from the Cross* (42) the monumentality and strictly central composition, symmetry and balance in the disposition of the figures, even their very foreshortenings, make one recall Michelangelo and Raphael, whose works had inspired Gossaert. At the same time the meticulous treatment of details, the pleasure taken in depicting ordinary objects, garments, jewellery, are evidence that the painter by no means had discarded his own national tradition. This painting is the central part of a triptych whose lateral leaves are at present in a collection in the USA.

The group portrait, coming into vogue in the sixteenth century, subsequently became very widespread in the north of the Netherlands.

45 (262)

46 (262)

Most of such works usually remained the property of the corporations and guilds which commissioned them and are to this day still found in the Netherlands. All the more then is the interest evoked by two pictures in the Hermitage by one of the founders of this genre, Dirk Jacobsz (c. 1497 – 1567), portraying a group of Amsterdam guardsmen (**43**).

Among the best pictures on display is *The Healing of the Blind near Jericho* (**44**) by Lucas van Leyden (1489/94 – 1533). In it Lucas van Leyden depicts the scene from the Gospel story which tells how Christ, passing near the walls of Jericho destroyed by the blasts of trumpets, saw a blind man and restored his eyesight.

The painter, in the manner of the Italian masters, skillfully singled out the main personages, and put them in the centre at some distance from the crowd. But of interest here is not so much the action, as the response to it. The attention, glances, gestures, are directed to the place where the miracle had taken place. On the whole the work is done as a genre piece, with the personages dressed as the painter's contemporaries; the colour scheme of the painting is bright and vivid, disclosing the strong influence of Netherlandish painterly traditions.

Though there are no paintings by the great sixteenth-century master Pieter Brueghel the Elder in the Hermitage, some idea of that painter's art can be gleaned from pictures by his son and pupil Pieter Brueghel the Younger (c. 1564–1638). *Kermis* (**46**), for a long time regarded as an original (which apparently has not survived) by Brueghel the Elder himself, gives one an idea of the early type of pictures painted by the great Netherlander when he frequently resorted to multifigured and small-figured compositions, depicting in great detail scenes from people's lives as observed from a distant and elevated point of view. The scenes consist of a whole number of individual episodes, each of them with a subject of its own.

There are many episodes in this picture as well, but singled out is the staging of the well-known story about the unfaithful wife caught by the husband, secretly brought home in a peddler's basket. Such works by Brueghel were justly called "encyclopaedias of Netherlandish life".

The Adoration of the Magi (**45**), which likewise, in addition to the main devotional scene inconspicuously tucked into a corner of the picture contains many episodes of city life, is noted for a splendidly painted winter landscape.

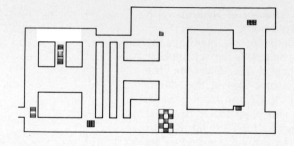

245   246   247

Flanders

47 (247)

The struggle of the Netherlands in the sixteenth century against Spanish domination and the feudal way of life resulted early in the next century in a division of the Low Countries. In the north an independent bourgeois state of Holland emerged, while the southern provinces, the largest of them Flanders, remained a dominion of the Spanish crown. The struggle for national independence and spiritual upsurge determined the flourishing of Flemish culture in the seventeenth century. Active in this period were Rubens, Van Dyck, Jordaens, Snyders and other outstanding artists. The Hermit-age possesses one of the world's finest collections of paintings by Peter Paul Rubens (1577 – 1640), the acknowledged head of the Flemish school. Rubens' dynamic style reached its climax in his huge decorative schemes for churches. In these works the artist elaborates on the heroic and noble deed, which opens the way to love and happiness.

In the picture *Feast at the House of Simon the Pharisee* (**47**), based on the scriptural subject (Luke 7: 47, 49), the dramatic conflict stems from the opposition of true faith and hypocricy. During the feast Simon the Pharisee and those who sat with him showed anger at Christ, who had allowed Mary Magdalene to wash his feet with her tears. Christ said: "Her sins, which are many, are forgiven; for she loved much."

The indignant reaction of the Pharisees, on the one hand, — "Who is this that forgiveth sins also?" — and the tranquil confidence of Christ and his disciples, on the other, are the picture's two poles. The movement from left to right, towards the figure of Christ, emphasizes the emotive centre of the composition.

In the creation of this picture Rubens was assisted by his pupils: Van Dyck painted the Apostle Peter and Jordaens the maiden in the upper part of the canvas.

One of Rubens' best works on mythological themes *Perseus and Andromeda* (**48**) was painted in the 1620s when his talent was at its height. Here the basic style asserted by the painter, namely Flemish Baroque, is quite prominent. The hero is an embodiment of the national ideal of male beauty and courage. He is a strong personality championing the cause of justice.

Rubens, who usually depicted dynamic scenes, this time preferred to

48 (247)

49 (247)

show the victor's triumph, rather than the actual battle in which Perseus slayed the sea monster and rescued the beautiful Andromeda. However, everything indicates that the passions stirred up by the battle have not yet abated. The figure of Perseus clad in glittering armour and a red flowing cloak seems to sweep forward; the wings of the mighty Pegasus stretch upwards and the Goddess of Glory, hovering above Perseus, is about to crown the victor with lawrels. The painter seeks to give the strongest impression of Perseus' manliness, strength, and vigorous temperament. This is why the bent legs of Perseus are exaggeratedly massive. In contrast, the nude figure of Andromeda is touchingly gentle and vulnerable. Her body reflects the pinkish, yellow and light blue highlights cast by surrounding objects. The shadows are transparent. Her body, illuminated by soft lighting, seems to be bathed in a golden haze.

Perseus is captivated by the beautiful Andromeda, and the love of the rescued princess is the hero's reward. Man gains happiness and freedom by struggle — such is the picture's optimistic message so much in tune with the sentiments of Rubens' compatriots.

An important place in the Hermitage collection is given to Rubens' sketches which fall into three groups: sketches for the large cycle of paintings on the life of Marie de' Medici; sketches for the decorations of Antwerp celebrating the state entry of the Cardinal Infante Ferdinand; and sketches

50 (247)

for individual paintings, such as *The Lion Hunt*.

Rubens' *Bacchus* (**49**), painted in the last years of his life, is one of the gems of the Hermitage collection. The great Flemish painter breaks the antique canons and shows the god of wine and merriment not as a graceful youth, but as a grossly obese man. This picture is a paean of human flesh.

The artist's talent as a portrait painter found vivid expression in the portrait of the *Lady in Waiting of the Infanta Isabella* (**50**). The strict lines of her dark dress and the rigid folds of the starched lace collar contrast with the young girl's fragile and poetic image and her dreamy grey eyes gazing into the distance. In this posthumous portrait of his daughter Clara Serena, who died

51 (246)

52 (246)

young, Rubens created a rare psychological image.

The art of Sir Anthony Van Dyck (1599–1641) is represented in the Hermitage by twenty-six pictures painted during the most important stages of his career. Among the early works created by Van Dyck in Antwerp *The Family Group* (**51**) is one of the best. The surface of the painting seems to vibrate and almost come to life due to light brushstrokes and grains of nearly dry pigments which combine with the texture of the partially unpainted canvas. The portrait conveys the spirit of a calm dialogue between the models and the viewer. We feel the attentive gaze of the woman, while her husband seems to be waiting for an answer from his partner whom we cannot see. This "im-mediate contact" between the sitter and the viewer was something quite novel for the time. Introduced by Van Dyck, it was repeatedly used by other artists.

Many of the Van Dyck pictures at the Hermitage belong to his English period, a time when, as Principal Painter to Charles I, he created numerous portraits of the king and members of the royal family and the aristocracy. Receiving countless commissions, Van Dyck frequently entrusted unsubstantial details to his pupils while he himself concentrated on the faces and other important elements of the pictures. But, of course, all the best works of this time belong entirely to Van Dyck's brush. Among them is the *Portrait of Sir Thomas Challoner* (**52**), one of the men who signed the death warrant of Charles I and who was banished from England following the Restoration. The picture is painted with light brushstrokes over a dense white ground in an almost sketchy manner which enhances the lively impression produced by a face no longer young.

Such masterpieces of Van Dyck's later period refute the opinion which alleged that the artist gradually departed from realism towards idealized representations characteristic of ceremonial portraits.

In his large formal portraits of Charles I (**53**), Charles' wife, Queen Henrietta Maria (**54**), the English courtiers Thomas Wharton and the Earl of Danby, Van Dyck combines virtuosity in conveying the model's individual features with a knack for

53 (246)

54 (246)

demonstrating the sitters' high social standing. Their dignity and official bearing are emphasized by their rich garments and faultless choice of accessories as well as by the vertical format of the pictures and elongated proportions, imparting the figures (intended to be viewed from beneath) grace and magnificence.

Van Dyck's ceremonial portraits evoked the admiration of contemporaries, who looked upon them as model portraits. Many painters, not only in England but in other European countries as well, strove to emulate his style.

One of the best religious compositions by Van Dyck is the *Virgin with Partridges* (**55**). It is based on the popular subject of the Rest on the Flight into Egypt and represents Mary, the infant Christ and St Joseph, amused by frolicsome *putti*. The scene is painted with the refinement and elegance which are so distinctive of this artist. Van Dyck, who never specialized in landscape, displayed in a number of his paintings, including this one, his brilliant potential as a landscape painter. Beautifully conveyed twilight and the picture's warm colours enhance the sensation of heart-felt intimacy. The painter resorts to the idiom of symbols, usual in his time: a sunflower always turning to the light is meant to signify the lofty thoughts of those portrayed; partridges, a symbol of debauchery, promptly fly away from the place where the holy family has settled down, etc.

Best known among the Hermitage works of Jacob Jordaens (1593 – 1678) is *The Bean King* (**56**), which depicts the Feast of the Magi as it was celebrated in Flanders of that time. A special pie was baked for the festivities, and the one who found a bean in his slice became the Bean King and everyone drank to his

health. In various pictures on this theme possessed by a number of museums Jordaens treats everyday motifs in a generalized and exalted manner. The markedly three-dimensional aspect of this figures in the foreground and a penchant for compositions overloaded with people and things depicted in close-up and from a low point of view are all characteristic of this artist.

At a time when most Flemish painters worked simultaneously in several genres, Frans Snyders (1579 – 1657) always gave preference to the still life. He was a virtuoso in painting the gifts of the earth, the water and the woods. Since human figures play

55 (246)

56 (245)

a secondary role in his pictures and were necessary only to impart to his still lifes a narrative element, he usually left their execution to his pupils. A large series of pictures of about the same format and of similar composition (*Shops*) were painted by the artist for the Bishop of Bruges. Very close in character to this series is the *Still Life with Game and a Lobster* (**57**). These decorative canvases, extolling the riches of the earth and sea, the beauty, abundance and variety of life, are executed in the Rubensian grand style.

Paul de Vos (1596–1678), the master of the still life and a noted animal artist, was a pupil and relative of

Snyders and learned a lot from him. His work is represented by impressive canvases full of dynamism and contrasts as, for example, *The Bear Hunt* (**58**). The painter depicts the moment of fierce combats between the hounds (in painting dogs he knew no rival) and wild beasts: a leopard, a stag, or bears. Depicting bodies entwined in struggle, at times with very complex foreshortenings, Vos builds a unified composition which always remains clear and expressive.

The landscape backgrounds in Vos' pictures are in all probability executed by Jan Wildens (1586–1653). This artist, who collaborated with

57 (245)

58 (245)

59 (248)

Vos and Snyders and worked in Rubens' workshop, is the author of the large-scale *Hunter with Dogs in a Landscape* (**59**), also in the possession of the Hermitage. Wildens demonstrates superb skill in representing both the winter scene and the group of figures. The contours of the trees are elegant, their dark silhouettes are bent in a typically Baroque manner and stand out against the snow-laden terrane. The grasses, stalks and leaves, which intertwine like the floral ornamentation of a tapestry, are particularly striking against the white snow. The diagonally built composition enhances the sense of motion. Wilden's picture is very decorative and may be easily imagined executed in tapestry form. Another version of the same picture, painted one year earlier, in 1624, is in the Dresden Gemäldegalerie.

The monumental works by the above-mentioned artists of the Rubensian trend sharply differ from paintings by their contemporaries Adriaen Brouwer and David Teniers the Younger, who preferred to paint pictures of smaller size and free of any monumentality.

Early in his career Adriaen Brouwer (*c.* 1606—1638) used to depict peasants and representatives of the lower strata of urban society — tramps and vagabonds. His pictures record the sides of reality which other Flemish painters hardly ever cared to paint. In the *Tavern Scene* (**60**), we see reckless drunks revelling in a shabby tavern. Depicted with realistic force they reveal the artist's gift for keen psychological observation. There are two sources of light, the window in the left foreground and the fireside in the right background, which help the artist organize the space and arrange the figures in it. The room, however, seems semidark and damp. The second Hermitage painting by Brouwer, *The Village Charlatan*, is also devoid of idealization: the painter depicts his "heroes" with

a touch of bitterness and irony. David Teniers the Younger (1610–1690), on the other hand, eschewed scathing characterization, always seeking to show what was pleasant or funny. His paintings with their somewhat idealized presentation of village festivals were a great success, and the Hermitage's picture *The Village Festival* (**61**) is a typical example of his manner. The painter skillfully incorporates amusing episodes featuring dancers, musicians, philanderers and rowdies into his clear-cut multifigured compositions. Teniers' versatility as a remarkable genre and landscape painter and animalist, master of the portrait

60 (245)

61 (245)

62 (245)

63 (245)

and still life, is confirmed by such pictures as the *Group Portrait of Members of the Antwerp Magistrate* and *Aldermen of the Marksmen's Guilds* (**62**), the magnificent *View in the Environs of Brussels*, the amusing *Monkeys in the Kitchen* (**63**), and *The Guard Room*, all of which are on display in the Hermitage.

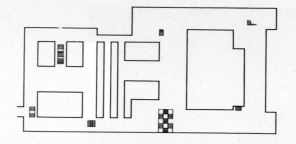

249

254

Holland

64 (249)   65 (249)

The Hermitage collection of seventeenth-century Dutch painting is one of the largest and most important in the world. In addition to a first-rate collection of paintings by Rembrandt, well represented in the museum are canvases by his pupils, as well as numerous works by nearly all the most famous painters who worked in diverse genres.

As a result of the bourgeois revolution in the Netherlands its seven northern provinces managed to liberate themselves in the early seventeenth century from Spanish domination, doing away with the feudal order, and creating what was then the most advanced state in Europe — the Republic of the Seven United Provinces, better known as the Dutch Republic.

The emergence of a new nation, and a new culture, and its economic burgeoning facilitated a florescence of the arts, painting in particular. In this small country with a population of no more than two and a half million, hundreds of artists were active. Many of them emerged as masters of world renown.

The Portrait of a Young Man Holding a Glove (**64**) and *The Portrait of a Man* (**65**) by Frans Hals (1582 – 1666) illustrate the new principles of representing the surrounding world on canvas, which were ascerted in the art of this seventeenth-century outstanding artist. He had a penchant for compositions conveying instantaneous expressions; he elaborated on a new technique of applying paint to canvas; he combined draftsmanship and painting within a single process; and he used open, free brushstrokes. In his portraits and genre paintings Hals vividly revealed the Dutch national character.

The widespread popularity of genre painting was one of the manifestations of the democratic tendency in Dutch art.

The pictures of a large group of genre painters, known as the Minor Dutchmen, were, as a rule, small in size, and were intended for decorating the interiors of ordinary town and country dwellers, reflecting everyday aspects of Dutch life.

Characteristic of the works by Jan Steen (1625/26 – 1679) is their engaging, at times even anecdotal, subject-matter. Such are *The Revellers*, *The Patient and the Doctor* (**66**), *A Game of Trick-track*. The painter combines a most meticulous treatment of detail with the composition as a whole, and is a superb master of light-and-shade and colour effects.

Pieter de Hooch (1629 – after 1684) and Pieter Janssens Elinga (1623 –

66 (249)

67 (249)

significant role in his pictures, emphasizing the foreground.

A major master of the "peasant" genre Adriaen van Ostade (1610–1685) in his early works poked fun at peasants, stressing their coarseness. The Hermitage possesses one of the best of them, *The Fight* (**70**), acquired by Peter the Great. In his later works the painter depicted peasants with greater understanding, recognizing their spiritual needs (*Village Musicians*). Under Rembrandt's influence the colours of Ostade's pictures became warmer, and there appeared a free play of light and dark over the canvas.

The still life became very widespread at that time. The term derives from the Dutch *still leven* which denotes a motionless (*still*) aspect of nature (*leven*), and very aptly reflects the

68 (249)

1682), both of whom worked at Delft, idealized urban life, reconstructing an atmosphere of tranquility and cosiness, the quiet and measured life of that little town. Both pictures, *A Woman and Her Maid in a Courtyard* by Hooch (**67**), and the *Room in a Dutch House* by Janssens Elinga (**68**), show a virtuoso rendering of atmosphere and lighting, which imparts a special expressiveness to the scenes depicted.

Evident refinement characterizes the works of Gerard Terborch (1617–1681). This painter has a special knack for setting off the beauty and special features of the texture of fabrics. He also displays great tact and elegant taste in his juxtapositions of colour. Notice especially *A Glass of Lemonade* (**69**) and *Reading a Letter*. Light plays a

69 (249)

character and content of the work by Dutch still-life painters. Attention should be given to pictures by Willem Claesz Heda (1594—1680/82) (*Breakfast with a Lobster*, **71**) and Pieter Claesz (1597—1661). Filled, apparently, with inanimate objects only — plates, wine glasses, dishes with foodstuffs — they by no means seem lifeless. Tableware pushed aside and a crumpled tablecloth, the

70 (249)

71 (249)

72 (249)

73 (249)

74 (249)

leftover wine in the goblets and the rind of the incompletely peeled lemon all indicate they were touched by human hands a moment ago. Heda, Claesz and other artists convey with meticulous authenticity the shape and three-dimensionality of objects, the texture of materials, reflecting light and colour on their surfaces.

On display are different types of still lifes — *Still Life with Fruits* by Balthasar van der Ast (1593/94 – 1657) (**72**), *Landed Fish* by Abraham van Beyeren (1620/21 – 1690) (**73**), and pictures representing other still-life subjects — trophies of the hunt, flower-pieces, etc.

The Dutch landscape and seascape are also well represented in the Hermitage. Jan Porcellis (*c.* 1584 –

1632) was an outstanding marine painter who depicted the sea as he saw it from the shores of Holland, masterly creating the impression of the restless elements of the waves, brisk wind and vast expanse (*The Sea on a Cloudy Day*, **74**).

In the tranquil pictures of Jan van Goyen (1596 – 1656), with their monochrome colour scheme, nature is closely linked with people (*The Shore at Scheveningen, A Winter View in the Environs of The Hague,* and others). The rendering of aerial perspective in the pictures of Jan van Goyen, Salomon Ruysdael and other artists was an important achievement of seventeenth-century landscape painting. Aert van der Neer (1603/4 – 1677), a landscape painter, specialized in moonlight effects. The chief

75 (249)

76 (249)

77 (254)

exponent of the animalistic genre, Paulus Potter (1625 – 1654), is represented by several canvases, including one of his best works, *The Farm* (**75**).

A profoundly philosophical interpretation of nature, clearly thought-out and expressive compositions – these are the trademark of the landscape painter Jacob van Ruisdael (1628/29 –

1682). Of the eleven of his paintings in the Hermitage *The Marsh* (**76**) is particularly well known.

The Hermitage collection of paintings by the greatest Dutch painter Rembrandt Harmensz van Rijn (1606 – 1669) includes twenty-four canvases.

In 1634, Rembrandt married Saskia van Ulenburch and created a number

78 (254)

of portraits of her. *Flora* (**77**) is
executed in the manner of a pastoral
portrait, fashionable at the time: in
it Saskia resembles an Arcadian
shepherdess with a spray of flowers
on the head and a wand entwined
with herbs and flowers. Rather than
seeking to portray the inner life and
character of his subject, Rembrandt
simply admires young Saskia in a
masquerade attire, delighting in the
rendering of decorative vestments,
which are dominated by cool
greenish tones.

Danaë (**78**) is among the most important creations of Rembrandt.
Based on the subject that was rather
common in the art of Renaissance
masters (Titian, Correggio), it was
reinterpreted by the Dutch artist

with freshness and originality. Whereas the Italians endowed Danaë with features of ideal beauty, emphasizing the erotic aspect of the myth, Rembrandt's message is of exalted feelings and the triumph of love. The artist's attention centers on the mood of a woman expecting her beloved. And the fact that Danaë's figure is not idealized imparts to the work a special human warmth, a special attraction.

David and Jonathan (**79**) is painted on a biblical subject. King Saul, jealous of David's greater popularity among the people than that of his son and heir Jonathan, decided to get rid of David. Before going into exile David, warned by Jonathan, weeps on the breast of his friend. Rembrandt's choice of this moment is not accidental. It was painted in the year his wife Saskia died, and the theme of people taking leave of their loved ones was apparently inspired by the artist's own personal tragedy. Therefore he gives Jonathan's face his own features, while David is depicted from the back so that one sees only the golden locks and a figure that might be associated with Saskia. People in the grip of profound emotion, the exotics of the Orient, gold-embroidered vestments brightly lit against the background of a dark, disturbing sky — all this puts the picture on a par with other works of Rembrandt painted in the 1640s in a manner which is conventionally called "Romantic".

More than half of the Rembrandt canvases in the Hermitage are portraits. Painted in different years they

79 (254)

make it possible to trace the evolution of portraiture in the artist's creative development. In the mid-1650s, he produced a number of so-called biographical portraits. He was particularly attracted by the faces of old people as they afford the opportunity to sum up the result of a lifetime (*Portrait of an Old Man in Red,* **80**; *Portrait of an Old Woman,* etc.).

Of Rembrandt's several pictures on the subject of the Holy Family, the version owned by the Hermitage (**81**) is the most important. Rembrandt transfers the scriptural figures into the setting of an ordinary house of a Dutch artisan — it was not for

80 (254)

81 (254)

82 (254)

famous canvases, *The Return of the Prodigal Son* (**82**). The parable of the son, who, unheeding of his father's admonitions, follows the path of sin and, eventually, having squandered his money and being reduced to tending a farmer's pigs, returns penitently home where he finds forgiveness, has been repeatedly represented in the art of many painters. Yet no one was able to interpret this subject so profoundly and wisely as Rembrandt.

It is not the adventures of the prodigal son, or the homily about the evil of profligacy that is the subject of this picture, but the tragedy of a wasted life, and readiness of people to help each other when in trouble. The lack of movement and outward distractions compels the onlooker to concentrate on the characters of the personages, on their emotive experiences. This masterpiece by Rembrandt, full of profound humanitarian meaning, can be regarded as a kind of summing up of the great master's creative life.

nothing that the picture was once called *The Carpenter's Family*. For all that, the painter is far from reducing his treatment of the subject to the level of a genre scene. Lively, intimate, executed in the golden tones characteristic of other Rembrandt canvases of the 1640s, with a bright red accent singling out the infant, the picture is captivating due to its homey narrative and, at the same time, to its exalted generalization. The artist applauds familial accord, creative effort and maternal affection.

Not long before his death Rembrandt finished one of his most

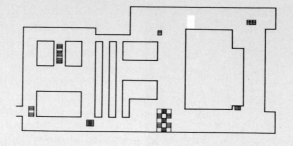

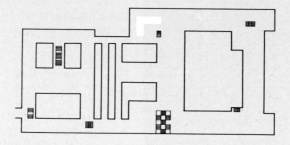

342

267   268

264

263

Germany

83 (263)

The collection of German painting at the Hermitage lacks works by such great masters as Albrecht Dürer, Hans Holbein the Younger and Grünewald, but the fourth great German Renaissance painter, Lucas Cranach the Elder, is represented by several works. In addition the collection has quite a number of splendid paintings by celebrated German painters of the seventeenth to the nineteenth centuries.

The display begins with fifteenth-century art.

The picture *The Last Judgement with Christ the Judge and Mary and John the Baptist* (**83**), executed in the early fifteenth century by an unknown artist of the Northern German school, is still closely linked with the Gothic tradition of the Middle Ages. Repre-

sentations of Christ against a gold background with a symbol indicating divine light (*mandorla*), and the smaller figures of Mary, John the Baptist and angels kneeling at his sides were traditionally placed above the entrance to churches.

The Hermitage picture was previously housed in the Townhall of Elbing and was used during sittings of the court for administering oaths. The wounds on Christ's hands and feet, as well as the scourge, lance and cross recalling his passion, and therefore his right to judge, are supplemented by other symbols — lilies (purity and innocence) and a sword (the power of justice).

The artist attempts to convey volumes by means of light-and-shade modelling, yet the line, contour and

84 (264)

silhouette are still of decisive importance in the picture. On the whole,
this work is an example of Late
Gothic art in the so-called "soft"
style (the blissful and sentimental
facial expressions, rounded folds of
the garments, etc.). An indication of
how highly the picture was valued
is the fact that it was presented by
the mayor of the city of Elbing
to Peter the Great for his wife.

85 (264)

Portrait of a Young Man (**84**) is the
latest of the surviving works of
Ambrosius Holbein (*c.* 1495 –
c. 1519), who died young, and
is among the best paintings of the
Hermitage's collection of German art.
The sitter is painted against an
architectural background, whose
many details – the gates, the tower
with the helmet-shaped dome, etc. –
resemble the fortifications of Milan
(it is quite possible that Holbein
travelled to Lombardy). The influence
of Italian art in Holbein's pictures
is evidenced also by meticulously
worked-out light-and-shade effects.
Renaissance features are manifested
also in the precise correlation of
the human figure with the architecture. An interest in the detailed
elaboration of architectural and ornamental motifs and a keen graphi-
cal manner are typical of the German
art of that time.

Notwithstanding the monograph on
the young man's beret and an indication that the model is twenty years
old, it has been so far impossible
to identify the sitter.

The picture *Venus and Cupid* (**85**)
by Lucas Cranach the Elder (1472 –
1553) was executed in 1509, a few
years after he settled at Wittenberg,
a seat of humanist and Renaissance
ideas. The painter found himself in
a humanist milieu and executed
predominantly secular commissions.
Venus and Cupid is the first representation of a nude goddess in
German art that has come down to
us, though, as known from historical
documents, images of nude antique
deities adorned the mansions of the

86 (264)

87 (264)

aristocracy as early as the fifteenth century.

In Germany the image of Venus assumed at times a formidable fateful character. Cranach did not deviate from this tradition. He found it necessary to invest the picture with an appropriate moral: "Resist by every means Cupid's temptations, lest Venus take possession of your blinded soul." This Latin verse is inscribed in the upper part of the canvas. But this admonition can hardly obliterate the sensual, earthly element characteristic of Cranach's picture.

Italian influence is also evident here in the painterly technique, in the modelling of the figures and in the dark background.

The best of Cranach's paintings in the Hermitage is *The Virgin and Child under an Apple Tree* (**86**). The Virgin in Cranach's interpretation is, above all, a symbol of repentance, rather than a personification of maternal affection as represented by Italian painters. In the Virgin Cranach embodies all the beauty of life and places her figure against the background of a cheerful landscape. The picture's content actually symbolizes the idea of Lutheranism (during the Reformation Cranach was friendly with Luther and was even called "the first Lutheran painter"). Mary is the second Eve who should redeem Eve's sin, just like Christ, who by his suffering redeemed the sin of Adam. The apple is a symbol of the Fall of Man, and the crust of bread in the infant's hands symbolizes Christ's body.

The sophistication of subject matter is characteristic of Mannerism which particularly influenced the later works of Cranach (*Portrait of a Lady*, **87**).

88 (267)

89 (268)

German art of the late sixteenth
and seventeenth centuries is represented by paintings done by a
number of major masters — Adam
Elsheimer, Hans von Aachen, Georg
Flegel, Johann Heinrich Schönfeld,
and others.

The activities of such well-known
painters as Daniel Schultz and
Antoine Pesne testify to the broad
ties of German art with the artistic
life of neighbouring countries in the
seventeenth and eighteenth centuries.
The German painter Daniel Schultz
(1615 — 1683), born at Gdansk, played
a notable role in the art of Poland
where he was a court painter to
Polish kings. In his *Family Portrait*
(**88**), formerly erroneously called the
*Portrait of a Mongol Merchant with
His Family*, the artist aimed at im-

mortalizing an important family
event, the bestowal of the title of
Grand Falconer on the elder son of
Prince Radziwill. Such a motif
is unique in art and has never
occurred in other paintings. What
imparts originality to this work is
the combination in it of the features
of the formal portrait (the figures
frozen in solemn poses, self-important
facial expressions, fashionable Polish
and French costumes) with the
authentic recording of the sitters'
prosaic, plain faces.

In his other formal portraits, too,
the German painter demonstrates his
close and keen study of the model,
without the least attempt at idealization.

90 (268)

91 (268)

Antoine Pesne (1683 – 1757), a Frenchman, was invited to Germany where for forty-three years he served as court painter to the Prussian kings. In his *Portrait of Dinglinger* (**89**) Pesne represented the famous jeweller at the court of the Elector of Saxony Augustus the Strong, a master whose works to this day take pride of place in the museums of Dresden, Potsdam and a number of other cities. Johann Melchior Dinglinger (1664 – 1731) appears in this official portrait clad in a rich costume, seated in an armchair and holding in his hand the Dianabad, a chalcedony bowl mounted in gold and silver. Set off against the semidarkness of warm and dark tones dominating the picture is the illuminated face of a confident man proudly displaying the magnificent creation

of his fantasy and craftsmanship. The Hermitage fund also contains a pendant portrait of Dinglinger's wife. Attention will also be attracted by the works of such well-known artists of the eighteenth and early nineteenth century as Anton Graff, Anton Kern, Angelika Kaufmann, which are on display in the rooms of German art.

Anton Raphael Mengs (1728 – 1779) was one of the most popular painters in eighteenth-century Europe. In the possession of the Hermitage are nine paintings which belong to his best works. The creative explorations of this artist, who was asserting the then new style of Classicism, were taken up not only in Germany, but in other countries as well wherever Art Academies emerged. Mengs adopted the theoretical views of the famous art historian Johann Joachim Winckelmann (1717 – 1768). His lasting stay in Italy, where the painter particularly admired monuments of classical antiquity and the work of Raphael, also profoundly influenced his paintings.

One of Mengs' best works, *Perseus and Andromeda* (**90**), was inspired by an antique cameo belonging to the painter's wife, now in the Hermitage collection. The subject comes from Ovid's *Metamorphoses* telling how Perseus rescued Andromeda, daughter of an Ethiopian king, from a seamonster. Mengs created a work based on logics and structural symmetry, on ideal proportions and precise draftsmanship. In this he was greatly assisted by a study of antique art: Perseus recalls to us the well-known

92 (342)

which is the replica of a self-portrait now at the Uffizi Gallery in Florence. Nineteenth-century German art is represented by a number of paintings by one of the outstanding German Romantics Caspar David Friedrich (1774—1840). In his landscapes he presents an emotive and poetical rendering of his country's nature. The artist conveys the grandeur of mountain landscapes (*Memories of the Riesengebirge, Morning in the Mountains*), the beauty of the moonlit sea near the coast (*Moonrise over the Sea*) or a view of the sea through the haze of a mist. The communion of man and nature is particularly keenly felt in his picture *On a Sailing Ship* (**92**). The seascape seems to be perceived through the eyes of the youth and maiden sitting on the prow of the sailing boat and admiring the spires and towers of a city which they are approaching through a foggy haze.

statue of the Apollo of the Belvedere, while Andromeda reminds us of the figure from the antique relief in the collection of the Museo Capitolino in Rome.

The painting, acclaimed by contemporaries, had quite a dramatic history of its own. Dispatched from Italy by sea to a client in England, it was captured by French pirates who attacked the ship and brought their booty to Cadiz in Spain. There it was purchased by the Naval Minister of France, and in 1779 was purchased for Catherine II.

On display is one of the Hermitage's two self-portraits of Mengs (**91**),

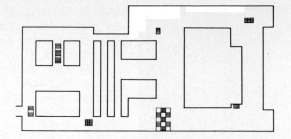

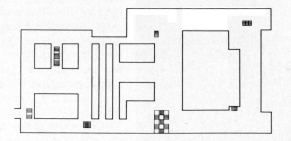

323 322
321
331 320
332 319
314 318
317
316

344
345

347
348
349
350

275
276

279
280

284
285

287
288

France

For its scope and quality of exhibits the collection of French art at the Hermitage is second only to the Louvre. The display occupies the rooms numbering from 272 to 297 on the first floor and the rooms 314 to 332 and 342 to 350 on the second floor.

The allegorical *Portrait of Anne of Austria* (**93**) by "the king's first painter" Simon Vouet (1590–1649) belongs to the period of the consolidation of French absolutism under the reign of Louis XIII. He depicts the queen of France as the Roman goddess Minerva. The language of allegory (the owl as the

93 (275)

94 (276)

95 (279)

symbol of Wisdom and laurels and staff symbolizing Glory and Authority), the cupids, the solemn decorations of the architectural backgrounds and intensive local colours – all this emphasizes the official character of the work intended to glorify royal power.

Realistic tendencies appeared in French painting of the seventeenth century in the work of the brothers Le Nain, Antoine, Mathieu, and Louis.

The Dairy Woman's Family (**94**) by Louis Le Nain (1593 – 1648), the most talented of the brothers, was painted in the 1640s. The figures here are immobile and seem to be disunited, yet they do form a monolithic group, magestic and monumental. This artist's work is based on a thorough knowledge of life, and every personage, therefore, is real and strictly individual. The peasants depicted are full of dignity, calm and confidence. The landscape is rendered by light, precise brushstrokes (the road is rendered by merely a single stroke). The fine colour scheme subordinates all the tints to a single silvery grey tonality.

The modest paintings of the Le Nain brothers, truthfully depicting scenes from peasant life, were an important contribution to the realistic trend in French painting.

The seventeenth-century painter of mythological subjects and landscapes Nicolas Poussin (1594 – 1665) embarked on another road, creating a new trend, Neoclassicism, in French art.

96 (279)

Poussin rejected genre painting, the representation of anything ordinary. He painted generalized, laconic forms for the unambiguous representation of ideas and, in so doing, leaned on Classical antiquity and on Raphael. In the picture *Tancred and Erminia* (**95**) Poussin takes up an episode from the poem *Jerusalem Delivered* by Tasso, telling how Tancred, severely wounded in battle, was saved by Erminia, who loved him. The artist attached great importance to the selection of a subject, and this theme, which in lyrical form glorifies self-sacrifice, was chosen deliberately. He depicted the moment when Erminia is cutting off her locks with a sword in order to bind Tancred's wounds with her hair.

The painter attracts attention to his personages in accordance with their importance by means of the principal colours — red (Tancred), blue (Erminia), and yellow (the knight's armour-bearer Vafrino). The participants in the scene are further characterized by their movements and postures: Tancred is elegant; Vafrino is the embodiment of concern; the light, almost soaring figure of Erminia is swift and impetuous. The uneasy red of the sky enhances the picture's emotional impact.

In his later period Poussin turned to landscape particularly often. In the *Landscape with Polyphemus* (**96**) he creates a majestic and beautiful image of nature. Hilly terrain with fields and a pond, groves and rocks soaring up to the skies is populated with both antique deities and mortals. The figure of the sad and lonely Cyclope Polyphemus seems to grow out of the rock on the crest of which he is sitting looking out into the distance where Galatea, who had captivated him, has disappeared. Nearby a ploughman is toiling, peasants are digging the earth, a shepherd is tending his flock. In this painting Poussin lauds the eternal harmony of life which he sees in the union of man and nature.

97 (280)

98 (284)

99 (284)

100 (284)

Poussin's art, which asserted humanistic principles, played a progressive role in the development of French painting.

Claude Lorrain (1600 – 1682), another leading exponent of the classical landscape, was famed for his ability to convey fine light effects and aerial perspective (*Morning*, *Noon*, *Evening*, and *Night* from the *Four Times of the Day* series). Quite representative in this respect is the picture *Morning in the Harbour* (**97**).

One of the greatest French artists Antoine Watteau (1684 – 1721) rejected traditional historical and mythological subjects in favour of real life which inspired him to paint actors, soldiers, landscapes and genre scenes.

Watteau's genre picture *A Savoyard with a Marmot* (**98**) in a lively and poetical manner presents the image of an itinerant young musician from the mountains of Savoy. With sincere sympathy for an ordinary human being Watteau transferred to canvas a scene gleaned from life.

Particularly popular were Watteau's paintings in the genre of so-called *fêtes galantes* (*An Embarrassing Proposal*, **99**). They hardly had any subject. Never imposing on the spectator any definite conclusions of his own, Watteau introduces him, as it were, into a world of poetic fancy and dreams. Ladies and gentlemen in costumes at times invented by the artist himself, are depicted in a conventional, idealized landscape, rendered in tiny vibrating brushstrokes. The surface of Watteau's paintings seems to scintillate due to subtle gradations of colour. The figures, arranged in a certain rhythmical unity, are light and graceful, their poses are elegant and mobile, the movements and glances are swift and fleeting.

In the *Capricious Lady* (**100**) the game of courtship with all its conventionalities is coloured with unaffected sadness and disappointment. The gliding patches of light and the delicate as lace folliage against the background of a bleakly yellow sky – all impart a special lyricism to the scene.

Whereas Watteau's refined and poetic art failed at times to appeal to the aristocratic circles of Paris, paintings by his follower Nicolas Lancret (1690 – 1743), depicting the more pleasant aspects of life and gladdening the eye, enjoyed a tremendous success. In addition to *scenes galantes* this painter was very fond of subjects from the theatrical world. Of his eleven canvases in the possession of the Hermitage the best known one is *La Camargo* (**101**), portraying a celebrated actress whose talent evoked the admiration of Voltaire, Grimm and other prominent personalities. Lancret depicts her during a performance on a park terrace. The airy landscape in the background adds to the sense of lightness created by the compositional structure of the picture. The eyes of the musicians around her follow her movements, emphasizing her dominant role. Her golden dress (in several other extant versions of the picture it is light blue) decorated with garlands of flowers in the

101 (285)

102 (285)

Rococo style also attracts the spectator's attention to the figure of the young ballerina, their warm colours contrasting with the pale blue sky. An outstanding artist working in the Rococo style which emerged in France in the mid-eighteenth century was François Boucher (1703 – 1770). A characteristic genre painting by this artist is the *Pastoral Scene* (**102**), which is hardly intended to be a record of the real life of French peasants. He places the scene in an elegant, fairy-tale setting. However, Boucher's gift of keen observation leads his brush to depict very con-

vincingly the seduction of a naive and simple-minded girl by the cunning tempter. Works by Boucher also demonstrate the painter's rich and varied talent as a decorator.

A major exponent of the new realistic trend in French art, associated with the ideology of the third estate, was Jean-Baptiste Siméon Chardin (1699 – 1779).

Scenes from everyday life and the still life – genres that were regarded as secondary in the art of absolutist France – come to the fore in his canvases. In such paintings as *The Laundress* (**103**) or *Grace Before Meat*

(**104**) Chardin contrasts the ideals of the aristocracy with those spiritual values which he discovers in ordinary town dwellers. He depicts their work, family relations, customs, the very setting and entourage of their day-to-day existence. In Chardin's small canvases with their special intimacy and gentle lyricism, rendered in warm, rich hues, the realistic traditions found further development and acquired new forms.

A pupil of Chardin and Boucher was the noted painter Jean-Honoré Fragonard (1732 – 1806). His best picture in this museum is *The Stolen Kiss* (**105**). The captured love scene is astonishingly lively. The painter demonstrates a virtuoso mastery of chiaroscuro, rendering remarkably well the texture of objects, notably that of shining fine fabrics, quite in the spirit of the Minor Dutchmen. How expressive, for instance, is the

104 (287)

103 (287)

striped scarf flowing after the girl's arm, emphasizing the movement and marking that diagonal which leads the spectator's gaze to the lovers' agitated faces. Without extending beyond the confines of the themes, characteristic of the Late Rococo, Fragonard vividly demonstrates his sincerity and his gift for keen observation.

The French Revolution of 1789 – 94 was a turning point in the history of the country which also transformed its art. The artistic movement which expressed the revolutionary aspirations of the progressive factions of French society was Neoclassicism, of which Jacques Louis David (1748 – 1825) became a leading exponent. Based on the political, philosophical and aesthetic tenets of the Enlightenment, the new art, with

105 (288)

106 (332)

its anti-feudal thrust, upheld man's social liberties, taking its heroic personages and subjects from antiquity.

Sappho and Phaon (**106**), the Hermitage's only work by David, was painted in 1809, during the First Empire period, at a time when the creator of the *Death of Marat* and portraits of revolutionaries had already abandoned the traditions of revolutionary Classicism.

The theme of this work is creativity inspired by love, as it depicts Sappho, the Greek poetess of antiquity, composing verse in praise of her lover Phaon. And though the painting lacks emotional spontaneity, the harmonious composition, its colouristic merits, the impressably precise draftsmanship — all testify to this painter's outstanding virtuosity.

David's pupil Antoine-Jean Gros (1771 – 1835), famous for his battle pieces, depicted in his *Napoleon at Arcole* (**107**) a real event of his time: during the battle of Arcole Napoleon carrying along his troops led an attack on the bridge defended by the Austrians. Gros depicted Napoleon alone, yet it seems that the general is in the thick of battle surrounded by a host of soldiers, and the portrait is perceived as a history painting. The figure's sharp diagonal turn, its expressive vitality, the banner fluttering in the wind, the contrasts of light and shade are just a few of the numerous features in this picture that run contrary to the rationalism and immobility of Neoclassicism, heralding the birth of the Romantic movement.

107 (314)

The head of the Romantic movement in France Eugène Delacroix (1798 – 1863) is represented in the Hermitage only by a sketch to *The Lamentation* and two small-scale pictures created towards the end of his creative career, *Lion Hunt in Morocco* (**108**) and *An Arab Saddling His Horse*. Painted more than twenty years after the artist's travels in Morocco and Algeria, they fail to faithfully recreate the realistic scenes witnessed by Delacroix and jotted down in his *Diary*. The painter strove above all to recreate the exotic nature of the Orient with its primeval nature, vigorous and bold people.

In his *Lion Hunt in Morocco* Delacroix rejected classicist canons and creates a dynamic composition unshackled by any rules. He further

108 (331)

109 (332)

enhances the impression by infring-
ing the laws of perspective, bringing
the background closer, distorting the
figures of the hunters, and produces
a sense of tension that precedes
dynamic movement. The painting is
executed in free brushstrokes. The
artist assigned the most important
function to colouring. He uses local colours, half-tones and reflexes,
attaining expressiveness by contrasting primary and complementary
colours. His pictures reveal his interest in the effect of light on colour
(the white shirt in the shade is rendered in green and blue tones).
All this helped Delacroix to enhance
the romantic quality of the work.

110 (323)

In the *Portrait of Count Guryev* (**109**) Jean August Dominique Ingres (1780 – 1867), a staunch adherent of Neoclassicism, depicts the Russian diplomat with the picturesque environs of Florence in the background conveying very authentically his facial features (the artist frequently painted plain faces hardly ever idealizing the model).

In spite of the features characteristic of Neoclassicism – a well-balanced centric composition, the triangular principle of its structure, dominant role of draftsmanship and smooth brushwork – this portrait betrays the Romantic striving for individual characterization, for enhancing the disturbed state of nature in anticipation of a storm and for creating the colour scheme of strong intensity. In opposition to classical conventions and also to Romanticism with its predilection for fantasy and exoticism, a realistic tradition began to assert itself in French art in the 1830s and '40s. A group of landscape painters led by Théodore Rousseau (1812 – 1867), united by their interest in landscape, set themselves the task of reflecting in their work the scenery of France. Having left their Paris workshops they settled in the small village of Barbizon on the outskirts of Fontainebleau in order to paint directly from nature. Hence their name, the Barbizon group.

A View in the Vicinity of Granville (**110**) shows the outskirts of a seaside town. The painter leaves the entire foreground almost deserted, painting in much greater detail the second plane, thereby drawing the spectator into the depth of the composition. This helps to create an impression of the God-forsaken spot lost among the rocks and wild groves. At the same time the painter reveals to the onlooker the peculiar charm of this unadorned spot of nature.

111 (323)

112 (323)

113 (322)

Though united by their love of nature, every member of the Barbizon group had a personal style and a preference for a particular type of landscape.

Characteristic of Jules Dupré (1811 – 1889) was a perception of nature more emotional than that of Rousseau. Rich in colours and executed in pastose brushstrokes, Dupré's pictures are an embodiment of nature's spontaneous force (*Village Landscape*, **111**, *Landscape with Cows*).

A romantic melancholy permeates the landscapes of Narcisse-Virgile Diaz de la Peña (1808 – 1876), half-deserted, with occasional trees and unconspicuous small figures of wayfarers (*Landscape with Pine*, **112**). The landscapes of Charles-François Daubigny (1817 – 1878), *The Banks of the Oise* (**113**), *The Pond*, *The Bank*, with their vast sky reflected in the waters of the river, are light and airy.

In one of the versions of the painting *On the Way to the Market* (**114**) Constant Troyon (1810 – 1865) displays his outstanding talent as an animal and landscape painter, conveying with virtuosity the movement of the herd in the haze of early morning.

The art of Jean-François Millet (1814 – 1875) is also associated with the village of Barbizon where he spent the last twenty-five years of his life. One of the major exponents of the French realist school, he revived the painting of peasant life started with the rustic pictures of the Le Nain brothers. He sees peasant life as a matter of heroic toil and

114 (322)

115 (321)

struggle. He sought, as he himself put it, "to draw man's thoughts to the sad lot of mankind and hard labour".

In Millet's *Peasant Women with Firewood* (**115**) the psychological characterization of the personages eclipses the genre subject of the picture. The artist concentrates on the slow, measured rhythm of the women's movement, bent under their heavy burdens. The subdued colouring, the composition with nothing that is inessential, and the generalized treatment of forms imbue the images of this small picture with severe monumentality.

The initiator of the "landscape of mood" in France was Camille Corot (1796—1875), an artist who painted also genre paintings and portraits. Corot's landscapes are imbued with the finest lyricism and harmony.

The Hermitage has seven of them, including the *Landscape with a Lake* (**116**), *A Peasant Woman with a Cow at the Edge of a Forest, Pond in the Woods, Landscape with Cows*, all of which provide an idea of the special characteristics of the artist's style. These small pictures depict quiet nooks of Île de France. The greyish silvery tonality, skillful utilization of values, the atmospheric effects — haze, mist, twilight — impart a special ethereal quality and charm to his canvases.

A new trend in French art which took shape in the 1870s was Impressionism. In distinction from the painters of the Barbizon School who executed their pictures in the studio after studies and sketches done from nature, the Impressionists exercised plein-air painting based on their immediate visual impressions. Claude

116 (321)

117 (319)

Monet may be regarded as the protagonist of this method.

The earliest of the eight Hermitage paintings of Claude Monet (1840–1926) is *A Lady in the Garden (Sainte-Adresse)* (**117**), painted in 1867. The painter conveys in a new manner the effect of daylight, registering not the actual colour of objects but that which can be seen at the given instant in the rays of the sun. Free, almost carelessly applied brushstrokes of pure colour convey the general impression of looking at a real landscape at a certain distance, in the light streaming through the air. *A Corner of the Garden at Montgeron* (**118**) with its uplifted mood and the *Haystack at Giverny*, depicted in the scattered light of a cloudy day, are both painted by separate brushstrokes of clear pigment to be optically fused in the eye of the spectator when viewed at a distance. The same features characterize other pictures by the Impressionists, such as, for instance, *The Boulevard Montmartre* by Pissarro, *Child with a Whip* by Renoir (**119**), and others.

In distinction from most of his Impressionist friends with a predilection for landscape, Auguste Renoir (1841–1919) more frequently painted figure compositions, nudes, and portraits. He combined plein-air painting with work in the studio. People and the joyous, brighter aspects of life were central in his art. In 1878, Renoir painted the *Portrait of the Actress Jeanne Samary* (**120**) in which his aim was not a profound psychological characterization. Rather, he sought to capture

118 (319)

119 (320)

120 (320)

the transient state of a given moment, nuances of sensation and mood manifested in a light movement, an incomplete gesture, the shadow of a smile, or a vivid glance.

Edgar Degas (1834—1917) hardly ever painted landscapes and worked only in the studio, from imagination or from memory. He had a predilec-tion for genre painting and for the portrait. Colour and drawing are of equal value in his paintings, while the preoccupation with light and air, so characteristic of landscape paint-ers, was of less importance to Degas. With enthusiasm he painted scenes from the life of contemporary Paris, depicting dancers on stage and in

121 (320)

122 (318)

the exercise room, horse racing, women at laundry, and so on. His keen interest in conveying movement, an expressive pose, a vivid gesture manifested itself in the creation of numerous nudes, frequently executed in pastel.

Two Hermitage pastels, *Woman at Her Toilette* and *After the Bath* (**121**), painted by Degas in the 1880s, show the artist's rejection of the academic tendency to idealize. Being true to nature is more important for him. He captures the fleeting movement seemingly at a glance, from an unusual point of view (from above or from aside). The singularity of this composition is emphasized by shifting the figure away from the centre or even "cutting off" part of it by the frame. Works by Degas astonish one by his unexpected and keen perception.

During the early stages of their careers such gifted artists of the late nineteenth century as Cézanne, Van

Gogh and Gauguin were influenced by Impressionism. Subsequently each of these Post-Impressionists developed their own individual manner. When creating new artistic forms they frequently departed from the habitual means of expression: they rejected linear perspective, resorted to the deformation of objects, enhancing the expressiveness of line and colour. But underlying all these departures was a profound understanding of the art forms of preceding schools. They sought monumentality, synthesis, decorativeness.

Paul Cézanne (1839 – 1906) shared the Impressionists' belief in the need to study nature, yet he never tried to capture the world's fleeting, momentary aspects. His purpose was to reveal such substantial qualities of objects, as volume, structure and weight, qualities which were lost in the Impressionists' paintings. Cézanne recreates reality in its material and structural essence, while organizing his paintings on the principle of colour contrast (which proved a further development and transforma-

123 (318)

124 (318)

tion of the Impressionists' method based on the dispersion of light).

Whereas in pictures by Claude Monet, for example in *A Pond at Montgeron*, the water is a shifty and variable element, in Cézanne's landscape *The Banks of the Marne* (**122**) it is static as a mirror and reflects the buildings and trees on the bank. The reflection, however, seems to belong to the same real, three-dimensional world. The tree contours in Monet's picture seem to dissolve in the shimmering sun-drenched atmosphere, while in Cézanne's canvas they are perceived as a single dense mass. Excluding from the landscape all incidental, transient elements, Cézanne creates a generalized and integral image of nature. Resorting to but a few colours (green, blue, orange and red) and juxtaposing

them to one another, the artist succeeded in suggesting space and volume.

In distinction from the Impressionists who very seldom painted still lifes, Cézanne worked a lot in this genre, but in his work he was guided by principles absolutely differing from those used by artists of preceding centuries. The world of objects regarded only as a superficial visual phenomenon held no interest to him. Resorting to simplification and certain geometrization, he sought to reveal the fundamental shape of objects and present them in a plastically clear image.

In the *Still Life with Curtain* (**123**) one hardly senses the freshness and aroma of the fruits, but each of them appears as part of a single objective world, possessing density, weight and volume. Unlike his predecessors, Cézanne did not use light-and-shade effects for such a presentation, but renders volume by modulating colour. His selection of paints enabled him to convey an object's contours without resorting for this purpose to drawing (for instance, orange-red fruits and white-bluish napkins in the *Still Life with Curtain*).

In his portraits Cézanne often approaches his sitter from the same positions as he did the still life, thus achieving in his images plastic expressiveness and sculptural clarity. In *The Smoker* (**124**), the generalization and simplification notwithstanding (for instance, there are no eyes — only dark spots), the artist shows a state of inner concentration; the

125 (317)

126 (317)

127 (316)

128 (316)

immobility of the peasant's figure is an embodiment, as it were, of the stability and constancy of provincial life.

The Hermitage possesses only late works by Vincent Van Gogh (1853–1890). Unlike the Impressionists, this artist did not seek to produce purely visual impression, but rather sought ways for conveying his own emotional state. His expressive means are intensified to the utmost: the heightened combinations of pigments enhanced the emotive qualities of the colour scheme, the drawing is expressive and tense and even the texture of the brushstrokes turns

into an effective means of conveying to the spectator the dramatic content and mood of the work.

These devices find their expression in the Hermitage pictures. In his canvas *Lilac Bush* (**125**) the artist seems to demonstrate the life of the plant in movement – its branching, growth, and flowering. The picture's blue-green colouring is astonishingly fresh. In the landscape *Cottages* (**126**) the expressive tension of the lines, the rushing brushstrokes, lay bare the artist's emotions and introduce a disturbing note into representations of a peaceful and charming village. The fifteen paintings by Paul Gauguin

129 (347)

130 (347)

131 (348)

133 (344)

the subordination of all the picture's elements to a well thought-out decorative pattern. He replaced light-and-shade effects and fine coloristic nuances by a harmony of pure colours, striving for expressive silhouettes and a rhythmical arrangement of lines. When creating his works he utilized only details of his studies from nature. Gauguin's art vividly manifested the tendencies inherent in the entire art of Post-Impressionism — monumentality, synthesis, imaginative generalization. The first artistic movement of the

134 (344)

(1848 – 1903) in the Hermitage's collection belong to the Tahitian period of his career. His departure for Polynesia and life there were something more than a kind of escape from civilization: the artist wished to experience the life and culture of other peoples. The pictures of the 1890s and the *Pastorales Tahitienne, Woman Holding a Fruit* (**127**), *The Idol* (**128**), all emerged as a result of a desire to comprehend the feelings of the Tahitians, understand their beliefs, their art and folklore. Yet they fail to reflect the actual life of the Maoris, rather demonstrating a poetical perception of such life and the artist's exaltation over the exotics of Tahiti.

Gauguin's peculiar manner consists in the generalization of forms and

135 (345)

136 (345)

twentieth century in France was Fauvism (from the word *fauve* — "wild", as the new trend was called by a hostile critic who visited the Salon d'Automne in 1905). Fauvism had no clear-cut theoretical platform, yet members of the group proclaimed independence from traditions and the right to follow their own inclinations; they indulged in an exaltation of pure colour to which they attributed prime importance. Their canvases are emphatically decorative. After the group fell apart, its members followed their own individual paths. The leading member of the Fauvists was Henri Matisse (1869 — 1954), who, according to his own words, sought ways of expression beyond the limits of literal copying.

Colour, rather conventional, but pure and unusually bright, particularly in juxtaposition to adjacent colour, plays a major role in his pictures. In order to enhance the brightness of his colour scheme the artist refrains from modelling forms and rendering various textures. He completely excluded light-and-shade effects and half-tones from his pictures. He also attributed great importance to lines formed by the borders of colour patches. They "build up" objects on a plane, delineate their contours, create movement, producing at the same time a decorative effect (as can be seen in *The Painter's Family*, *The Red Room*, **129**, *Conversation*, **130**, *The Dance*, **131**, *Music*, *Portrait of Mme Henri Matisse*, **132**). Matisse transforms the traditional elements in the compositional structure of a painting or rejects them altogether which approximates some of his works to decorative panels — there is no depth of space, his forms are simplified and schematic. Even in the pictures where seemingly nothing happens, where people and objects are just side by side, the interaction of lines and colours give birth to their inner bonds.

Matisse's thirty-seven paintings in the Hermitage were all created before 1914; they provide a vivid and complete idea of his joyous, life-asserting works.

The museum possesses a vast collection of paintings by Pablo Picasso (1881 — 1973) as well; yet all his paintings, of which there are also thirty-seven, belong to his early period. The art of this painter is complex and varied, reflecting the sharp contradictions of the twentieth century. Well versed in the cultural traditions of the past, of Spain (his native land) in particular, Picasso arrived at the turn of the century in Paris, a city that played a vanguard role in the artistic life of the time, to seek new paths in art.

The earliest dated painting of Picasso in the Hermitage is *The Absinthe Drinker* (**133**); together with a number of other works belonging to his Blue Period (1901–4) and the subsequent Rose Period (1904–7), it shows the artist's interest in the destiny of the poor, his sympathy with their loneliness and sufferings. Even in pictures in which Picasso

138 (349)

turns to themes no longer new in French art, as, for instance, the cafés and their customers, reality is presented in a conventionally transformed aspect. Looking at the personages of his pictures executed in those years, it is usually difficult to say who these people are and to what country or time they belong. However, the generalization evident in the treatment of images impart to them an expressiveness, while the deliberate deformation of the figure and conventional colour enhance drama and the emotive impact of the works.

Belonging to the Rose Period is the lyrically sad *Boy with a Dog* (**134**), done in gouache. The pink and light blue tones, the delicate drawing with soft, smooth contours, enhance the impression of naturalness and movement in the scene. There are no innovations in this

137 (349)

139 (349)

canvas, as Picasso at this stage does not yet break out of the pictorial traditions of nineteenth-century art. Quite different tendencies appeared in Picasso's works when he emerged as one of the founders of a new movement in twentieth-century art, that of Cubism. In 1908, the adherents of this movement united in the Bateau-Lavoir group. The collection of Picasso's pictures at the Hermitage makes it possible to trace the artist's two periods in the development of Cubism – analytical and synthetic. In the former Picasso sought to reveal the inherent structure of the human figure or material objects. In *Woman with a Mandolin* (135), painted in 1909, objects as such are still there yet the visual aspect of reality is not directly transferred to canvas. The artist expresses his ideas by reducing all forms to geometrical schemes.

During the second period Picasso breaks down form into its constituent elements which he then unites in complex rhythmical compositions (*Musical Instruments*, 136). In 1914, Picasso departed from Cubism and subsequently his art developed along different paths.

The art of the major French landscape painter of the twentieth century

140 (349)

141 (349)

Albert Marquet (1875 — 1947) is notable for its great integrity. He was
able to combine innovation with
adherence to realistic traditions.
A short-lived affinity with the
Fauvists inspired him towards generalization, bright colour patches and
restrained contours. Among his im-
mediate impressions from nature he
selected the most important and
concentrated attention on it. The
artist restricted his pictorial means
so much that his pictures are usually rendered in a single tonality.
Marquet's landscapes are always very
precise as to season of the year, time
of day and weather conditions, and,
most importantly, truthfully convey
the city's very individual atmosphere.
Marquet depicts well-known places
in Paris (*Holy Trinity Square*, **137**,
*View of the Seine with the Monument
to Henri IV, A Rainy Day in Paris*,

138) and other cities (*Hamburg Port*,
139), but his canvases always evoke
a sensation of freshness, innovation
and poetry.
The five works by the outstanding
French painter of Dutch origin Kees
van Dongen (1877 — 1968) belong to
the period of Fauvism. Van Dongen's
subjects often come from the Montmartre where he gained inspiration
while observing the life of actors,
frequenting the cafés and the circus.
One of his favourite subjects are
dancers. These images have acquired
a special quality distinctive of his
manner alone. He was able to show
the inner energy and temperament of
his models, the hot breath of a dance,
and the sensuality underlying it.
The painter used the potential of

142 (349)

143 (350)

144 (350)

artist created another vivid and colourful canvas, though his expressive means have somewhat changed. Enhanced is the graphic element, the contour; there appears an interest in ornamentation which foreshadows a transition to the Arabesque, characteristic of Van Dongen's later manner.

The Hermitage's fourteen canvases by André Derain (1880 – 1954) were painted by the artist before the First World War, in the period when his art flourished. One of the founders of Fauvism, initially very close to Matisse, Derain subsequently more than once changed the character of his paintings.

The Harbour in Provence (Martigues) (**143**) reveals his striving towards simplification and enlargement of forms (large tree in the foreground, hills and mountains, clearly delineated walls and roofs of houses densely crowded in township). Derain was obviously under the spell of the Primitives, when he painted the trees scattered over the hillside as if ornamental spots, clumps of grass and clouds resembling white birds, all of similar shape. Parts of the canvas left without paint also help in creating an impression of the painter's seeming unprofessionalism, though in fact they intensify the lighting, changing and enhancing the perception of colour.

What is new and unusual in Derain rests on his excellent knowledge of classical traditions, convincingly confirmed by the well-built composition with a forefront which leads the spectator's eye back into the picture's

colours boldly and in a new way. In *The Red Dancer* (**140**) colour becomes the principal means of expression – the bright, flaming paints applied in free broad brushstrokes not only convey forms and movement, but create an emotional whirlwind which rarely fails to captivate the onlooker.

A high-key colour scheme dominated by green imparts special beauty to the *Lady in a Black Hat* (**141**) in which Van Dongen embodied his idea of an exalted, somewhat mysterious and romantic image of a Parisienne. In *Lucy and Her Partner* (**142**) the

145 (350)

treated figure and face evoke associations with African plastic art. Using deformation and grotesque, the artist makes a step in the search for expressiveness.

Represented among the works of twentieth-century French artists are pictures by Fernand Léger (1881—1955), an artist whose talent reveals itself in monumental painting, mosaics, stained glass and pottery as well. After a brief association with Cubism and remaining an adherent of conventional images and devices in composing his pictures, Léger never lost his positive, life-asserting attitude toward the surrounding world. His *Carte postale* (**145**) is a complex composition of clearly arranged parts and rhythmical repeats. Despite its seemingly fragmentary nature, it presents an integral image, monumental and optimistic.

depth, by the arrangement of voluminous masses in the form of coulisses and by the diagonal of the canal with the sailboat gliding on it, stressing the effect of recession into space.

The Portrait of an Unknown Man with a Newspaper (Chevalier X) (**144**) reminds one of pictures painted in the traditional manner, particularly formal portraits, in which the sitters were also depicted exquisitely attired, in a sumptuous interior with marble-flagged floors, often in an arm-chair against the backdrop of a curtain, tied for effect with a cord. It is such a comparison with the habitual that enhances the feeling of Derain's unusual design. The sitter's schematically and simply

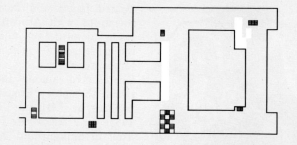

197

299

300   301

England

The Hermitage's comparatively small collection of British art is dominated by portraiture and landscapes. In addition to works by such great masters as Reynolds and Gainsborough, on display are many paintings by other well-known artists: Romney, Lawrence, Wright, Morland and Dawe. The subject of the painting *The Infant Heracles Killing Snakes* (**146**) was taken by Joshua Reynolds (1723 – 1792) from the antique Greek poet Pindar. Heracles always lived in the shadow of Hera's hostility, because he was the offspring of one of the many infidelities of her husband Zeus. While he was still an infant she sent two poisonous snakes into his room at night, but he picked them up, one in each hand, and

146 (299)

147 (299)

fee, she sent the painter as a gift a diamond-studded snuffbox with her portrait.

At the same time Reynolds created two other paintings commissioned by Grigory Potiomkin, a favourite of Catherine II: *The Continence of Scipion Africanus* and *Cupid Untying the Zone of Venus* (**147**). Even though the Hermitage has no portraits by Reynolds, the collection provides an idea of the high standards of portrait painting attained in England, where the genre flourished in the seventeenth and eighteenth centuries.

The name of the beauty painted by Thomas Gainsborough (1727—1788) in the *Portrait of a Lady in Blue* (**148**), is unknown. The calm pose, elegant gesture, spirited face emphasize the nobility and refinement of this young and charming woman. The combination of the pink tones of the face with the silvery grey, white, and blue tones of the powdered hair, dress and shawl is exquisite. Gainsborough was a brilliant colourist. His special manner of applying fluid paints in a semitransparent layer thus giving the impression of airiness and lightness, his rapid strokes made with a fine brush, his predilection for half-tones — all this imparts to his images a poetic quality and elegance. Gainsborough's only work in the museum is the best of all the English pictures in its possession.

Among the first-rate works of the Hermitage collection is the *Portrait of Mrs. Harriet Greer* (**149**) from the brush of Georges Romney

strangled them, thus allaying the anxiety of his alarmed mother, Queen Alcmena.

Many faces in the picture are the likenesses of people the artist actually knew. In the old man, the prophet Teiresias, who prophecied the greatness of Heracles, contemporaries recognized Reynolds' friend, the lexicographer Samuel Johnson, and the goddess Hera, watching the working of her revenge from high in the clouds revealed a likeness to the famous English actress Sarah Siddons. The large scale of the composition, the diversity of foreshortenings, the contrasts of light and shade and other devices of Baroque art were skillfully used in this painting.

Catherine II highly appreciated Reynolds' work and hung his picture in the Hermitage. In addition to his

148 (300)

149 (299)

150 (300)

(1734—1802). In depicting his model, the artist concentrates on conveying her beauty and charm, rather than giving a conscious comment of character. Conceived as a formal portrait, it nevertheless evokes a sensation of freshness and naturalness enhanced by the asymmetry of the composition and by the light and broad painterly manner. Rendered in free brushstrokes are the curls of the fashionable hairdo, the semitransparent fabric covering her breast, the feathers adorning the hat. The broad brim of this black hat, just as the dark clothing, effectively set off the woman's handsome face with its smooth skin and attentive gaze turned towards the spectator.

Joseph Wright of Derby (1743—1797) gained fame for his skillful rendering of the complex effects of light. His two pictures in the Hermitage, *The Blacksmith Shop* (**150**) and *The Annual Girandola, Castel Sant' Angelo* are typical examples. Particularly striking is the *Blacksmith Shop* which attracts the onlooker with its romantic mysteriousness, bold contrasts, and the juxtaposition of different sources of light (the moon in the night sky shedding its cold light, the warm flashes from the fire of the forge concealed behing the dark silhouette of the busy smith, the burning candle and the light outside the windows).

When painting such pictures, the artist, partitioning off differently illuminated parts of his studio by a system of black screens, watched from the darkness the illuminated objects and rendered them on canvas.

Paintings by Wright enjoyed tremendous success and were frequently repeated by him. Several times he painted variations of *The Blacksmith Shop*, and repeated *The Annual Girandola* about twenty times. Although among the English landscapes in the Hermitage collection there are none by Thomas Gainsborough, who was also a major landscape painter, there are on display landscapes by other well-known English artists, including George Morland (1763 – 1804). The motif rendered in his *Approaching Storm* **(151)** in all probability was of great interest to the artist for he turned to it several times, imbuing his pictures with an element of romantic emotiveness and disquiet. The small figures of the traveller and his horses and dog discomfitted by the approaching storm are depicted in sharp contrast to the natural elements – the enormous darkened sky with swiftly moving storm-laden clouds and the branches of the bushes bent by gusts of wind. The diagonal division of the composition, the contrasts of light and darkness enhance the drama of the scene.

151 (300)

152 (301)

military uniform studded with decorations, and lastly, the massive handle of the sword – all sum up the character of a successful statesman, general and aristocrat.

Especially numerous in the Hermitage are portraits coming from the brush of George Dawe (1781 – 1829), who spent the last ten years of his life in St Petersburg where he arrived at the invitation of the Emperor Alexander I for creating a portrait gallery of the generals – heroes of the war against Napoleon. In Russia he received commissions from other

153 (197)

Outstanding among the masters of the first third of the nineteenth century are Thomas Lawrence and George Dawe.

The Portrait of Count Mikhail Vorontsov (**152**) is one of the four paintings by Thomas Lawrence (1769 – 1830) possessed by the Hermitage. Though comparatively small (canvases of a much larger format were frequently used in British formal portraiture), the picture gives the impression of grandeur and magnificence. This is further set off by the vertical composition and the depiction of the model from a low viewpoint, so that the figure, clearly delineated against the background of the sky, appears to be almost sculptural and monumental.

The proud turn of the head, the hand firmly clasping the glove, the cloak thrown over a shoulder, the

154 (197)

persons as well, yet the bulk of his works in the museum will be found not in the rooms displaying British art but in the 1812 War Gallery of the Winter Palace.

Owing to the fact that at the time when the paintings were being done some of the 1812 war heroes were no longer living, Dawe at times had to use portraits by other painters. Thus, when doing the full-length portrait of General-Fieldmarshal Mikhail Golenishchev-Kutuzov (153), Dawe painted his head from a portrait executed from the life by Volkov. He represented the Commander-in-Chief of the Russian Army under a fir-tree against the background of the snow-clad plains of the battlefield.

The portrait of Kutuzov's predecessor as Commander-in-Chief, General-Fieldmarshal Mikhail Barclay de Tolly, who later, in 1813–14, com-

manded the troops, was painted in a similar way, with the face being reproduced after a portrait by Zenf. But, of course, the best idea about Dawe's painterly talent comes from the portraits he painted from the life. Among them is the remarkable *Portrait of Alexei Yermolov* (154) whose figure is presented in a bold and unexpected turn, virtually with his back to the spectator, and the face seen in profile. The General's stern profile stands out clearly, as if cast of bronze, against the dark background. His face, with eyes sparkling from under knitted eyebrows and firmly compressed lips, and locks of hair fluttering in the wind give the impression of energy, strength and iron will. This portrait evoked the admiration of the poet Alexander Pushkin who noted that when Yermolov frowned he looked exactly the way he was depicted by Dawe.

In this, just as many of his best works, Dawe demonstrated not only his skill as a painter of formal portraits, but also his keen power of observation, the ability to reveal his sitters' character.

Index of Artists Whose Works Are Reproduced in the Present Volume

Roman figures refer to pages, those in italic to illustrations.

* Number 78 is now under restoration.

Useful Information

Address: 36 Dvortsovaya Naberezhnaya (Main Entrance of the Winter Palace)

Telephones: Director 2198615, 2198604; Inquiries 2198625, 3113465 (intercom 525); Excursion Bureau 3113420; Administrator 2198657 (intercom 857). Open every day, from 10.30 a. m. to 6 p. m.; closed Monday. Tickets are sold in the Main Entrance Hall. The sale of tickets is discontinued one hour before closing time.

ГОСУДАРСТВЕННЫЙ ЭРМИТАЖ, ЛЕНИНГРАД

КАРТИННАЯ ГАЛЕРЕЯ.

Путеводитель (на английском языке)

Издательство «Аврора». Ленинград, 1989

Изд. № 1631. (2 — 60)

Типография ВО «Внешторгиздат», Москва

Printed and bound in the USSR